T0074948

AI BY DESIGN

CHAPMAN & HALL/CRC
ARTIFICIAL INTELLIGENCE AND ROBOTICS SERIES

Series Editor: Roman Yampolskiy

Artificial Intelligence Safety and Security
Roman V. Yampolskiy

Artificial Intelligence for Autonomous Networks
Mazin Gilbert

Virtual Humans
David Burden, Maggi Savin-Baden

Deep Neural Networks
WASD Neuronet Models, Algorithms, and Applications
Yunong Zhang, Dechao Chen, Chengxu Ye

Introduction to Self-Driving Vehicle Technology
Hanky Sjafrie

Digital Afterlife
Death Matters in a Digital Age
Maggi Savin-Baden, Victoria Mason-Robbie

Multi-UAV Planning and Task Allocation
Yasmina Bestaoui Sebbane

Cunning Machines
Your Pocket Guide to the World of Artificial Intelligence
Jędrzej Osiński

Digital Afterlife and the Spiritual Realm
Maggi Savin-Baden

A First Course in Aerial Robots and Drones
Yasmina Bestaoui Sebbane

AI by Design
A Plan for Living with Artificial Intelligence
Catriona Campbell

For more information about this series please visit:
https://www.routledge.com/Chapman--HallCRC-Artificial-Intelligence-and-Robotics-Series/book-series/ARTILRO

AI BY DESIGN

A PLAN FOR LIVING WITH ARTIFICIAL INTELLIGENCE

CATRIONA CAMPBELL

CRC Press
Taylor & Francis Group
Boca Raton London New York

CRC Press is an imprint of the
Taylor & Francis Group, an **informa** business
A CHAPMAN & HALL BOOK

First Edition published 2022
by CRC Press
6000 Broken Sound Parkway NW, Suite 300, Boca Raton, FL 33487-2742

and by CRC Press
4 Park Square, Milton Park, Abingdon, Oxon, OX14 4RN

CRC Press is an imprint of Taylor & Francis Group, LLC

© 2022 Catriona Campbell

Reasonable efforts have been made to publish reliable data and information, but the author and publisher cannot assume responsibility for the validity of all materials or the consequences of their use. The authors and publishers have attempted to trace the copyright holders of all material reproduced in this publication and apologize to copyright holders if permission to publish in this form has not been obtained. If any copyright material has not been acknowledged please write and let us know so we may rectify in any future reprint.

Except as permitted under U.S. Copyright Law, no part of this book may be reprinted, reproduced, transmitted, or utilized in any form by any electronic, mechanical, or other means, now known or hereafter invented, including photocopying, microfilming, and recording, or in any information storage or retrieval system, without written permission from the publishers.

For permission to photocopy or use material electronically from this work, access www.copyright.com or contact the Copyright Clearance Center, Inc. (CCC), 222 Rosewood Drive, Danvers, MA 01923, 978-750-8400. For works that are not available on CCC please contact mpkbookspermissions@tandf.co.uk

Trademark notice: Product or corporate names may be trademarks or registered trademarks and are used only for identification and explanation without intent to infringe.

Library of Congress Cataloging-in-Publication Data
A catalog record has been requested for this book

ISBN: 978-1-032-21152-7 (hbk)
ISBN: 978-1-032-19666-4 (pbk)
ISBN: 978-1-003-26700-3 (ebk)

DOI: 10.1201/9781003267003

Typeset in Joanna
by codeMantra

CONTENTS

AUTHOR

Catriona Campbell currently works at one of the world's largest professional services firm as the UK company's first-ever Client Technology and Innovation Officer. She holds degrees in Psychology and has a particular interest in the field of Human–Computer Interaction – the discipline where Psychology meets Technology to design better systems. After university, Catriona joined Barclays, becoming its first Head of Digital. Showing a tremendous knack for timing, she founded her UX and Experience Design start-up in London just before the dot-com bubble burst in 2000. After surviving then prospering, the agency was sold in 2015 to one of the world's largest Management Consultancies. Catriona has spent over 20 years working with customers to co-create new digital innovations. She is passionate about storytelling, delivering great customer experiences and counts herself fortunate enough to have worked with companies like Barclays, Sky, Vodafone, Skype, Dell, Heineken and Microsoft.

Catriona has lived and worked globally and led project teams in all six continents. She has three wonderful children, two dogs, one husband and a small flock of chickens. The UK government asked her to work on their first Usability & Accessibility standards in 2005. In 2012, she was voted into the BIMA Digital Hall of Fame along with Sir Tim Berners-Lee and Sir Jony Ives. She is currently helping the Scottish Government's AI strategy.

ACKNOWLEDGEMENT

Welcome to *AI by Design: A Plan for Living with Artificial Intelligence* – my first book! I am excited for you to read it, hopefully, learn something new and be entertained whilst you do it. I've spent about 25 years working in technology, and in the early days, I wrote articles and presented at conferences about things I knew, deeply, from my own experience. About 5 years ago, I got equally concerned and excited about AI, so much so that I began to write about it. To a relative newcomer, this was a different experience, I felt uncomfortable not being the expert and imposter syndrome kicked in. As I descended into an increasingly deep AI research blackhole, I learnt that the more I understood, the less I knew. This made it worse. But then, I realised that AI is too big for anyone to grasp entirely and found that my experience in design, psychology and business transformation is a benefit. I could look at the challenges from the perspective of someone who has made big technology changes happen. I found my voice. So, after annoying my children with the phrase (from the amazing Netflix documentary) "we need to talk about AI," I decided that I do. So I have!

The goal of the book is to share my thoughts and experiences on a serious topic. I've always loved storytelling to bring potentially dry subjects to life, so I've included tales from our recent past. Human history has a habit of repeating the same patterns of behaviour and if we listen, we can learn from our mistakes. I like people, so have told their stories when I think it helps. There are also five fictional tales on potential future scenarios with AI, which I hope you'll enjoy.

So, after a long journey here we are, in print, on your kindle (other devices are available) and already thinking what's next. But before that, I'd like to make a few thank you's to recognise those who have helped me along the way. A book takes a long time to write and get published and it truly is a team effort. Thank you to Steven Allison for his help in researching and drafting, and his great ideas and eye for a story. My husband Sion deserves a medal for his historical knowledge, editing, patience and for hunting down a publisher. They're an elusive quarry. Still waiting for some agents to respond a year later. Thanks to my editor Elliott Morsia for believing in the book and for CRC Press/Taylor & Francis Group for publishing. Thank you to my parents, Marie and Colin for giving me a wonderful childhood, allowing me to travel and open my eyes to the world. My brother Grant was my first Marketing Manager and is now an amazing Creative Director – I was so lucky to have his support. Thanks to my children for listening to my stories.

Thank you for reading.
Catriona Campbell

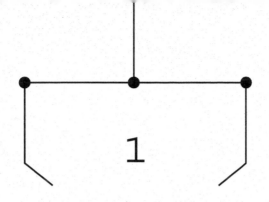

SLEEPWALKING INTO SINGULARITY

The important thing is not to stop questioning. Curiosity has its own reason for existence.

Albert Einstein, 1955, *Life Magazine*.

WHAT IS ARTIFICIAL INTELLIGENCE?

You'll find Artificial Intelligence (AI) used every day, all over the world, and you probably don't even realise how much. AI is used to recommend what series you binge next on Netflix, answer your customer service queries in a chatbox or flag the potentially revealing photo you just uploaded on Tinder. Siri's AI listens to your voice, Facebook's algorithms decide what stories you see and an AI might even manage your pension fund.

So, consciously and unconsciously, we are using AI-driven software and apps every day. However, AI is poorly understood and not just among the general public. Even in the business world, where AI powers some of the most disruptive technologies, few have a profound, firm grasp of AI, although AI has been around far longer than the age of social media. In 1956, John McCarthy, one of AI's founding fathers, co-authored a proposal that coined the term "artificial intelligence," referring to machines thinking for themselves. He defined AI as: "The science and engineering of making intelligent machines, especially intelligent computer programmes."

DOI: 10.1201/9781003267003-1

As Moore's Law has attested, computing power has doubled every year since 1960 (although this appears to be slowing down), so hardware and cloud computing capabilities are powered up and ready for the massive computational power needed by AI. The first generation of modern AI is called 'Narrow-AI,' such as Netflix recommendations or automated chatbots. Using machine learning (ML) to teach itself by feeding lots of information about one task, narrow-AI will continuously hone its accuracy. They don't have general intelligence like humans and can only work on that particular task.

Coders design narrow-AI to be benign, and although not all are as friendly as Siri, you still may want to consider sleeping with one eye open. Why is that? Because Norman the world's first AI psychopath could sneak into your bedroom in the dark of night! Fortunately, I'm kidding about Norman coming to get you, as he's just like any other narrow AI and can only do one job. And in this instance, Norman's only capability is image captioning, a popular method of creating a text description of an image. Researchers at MIT's Media Lab trained Norman (named after Norman "Psycho" Bates) by showing him lots of pictures that he learnt to describe himself. Exposing Norman to gruesome and violent content from the internet, the researchers demonstrated how easily AI algorithms can end up biased. For instance, while a standard AI could describe one inkblot image as "a close up of a vase of flowers," Norman would say it's "a man is shot dead" or the example below:

INKBLOT #4
Norman sees:

"MAN GETS PULLED INTO

DOUGH MACHINE."

INKBLOT #4
Standard AI sees:

"A BLACK AND WHITE

PHOTO OF A SMALL BIRD."

Inkblot. (MIT Media Lab, 'NORMAN: World's first psychopath AI,' Pinar Yanardag, Manuel Cebrian, & Iyad Rahwan.)

You see, it doesn't take much to twist narrow-AI into something more sinister. Facial recognition technology and Deepfakes are just two examples of the potent narrow-AI technology in its infancy. Let's take a look at Deepfake technology which is already readily available to create convincing fakes of public characters. Deepfakes are created by taking original video or photo imagery and applying them to an online dummy – ML then continuously tests how the Deepfake looks compared to the original until it's perfect. The 2020 United Kingdom Alternative Queens speech showcased Queen Elizabeth being Deepfaked. The narrow-AI technology copied her voice, movements and surroundings, so some viewers may have thought the Queen was real, probably until she began to dance on the table.

Counterfeiting products is nothing new in the world. Fake hand-bags, whisky and pirate software are all big 21st-century businesses. If every Louis Vuitton bag carried on the high-street was genuine, then it would be a mainstream brand! Companies use security teams and digital tools to protect their intellectual property and balance the cost of policing their brand against the benefit. Criminal gangs are often responsible for churning out replica physical goods by the thousand. Such crimes are often overlooked and only tackled when a local police crackdown occurs, or a large shipment is uncovered. Even so, there is risk selling physical products and the cost of producing or 'procuring' the fake goods. Digital counterfeiting is the new game in town.

Digital copying of software, piracy of movies and music have been around since the turn of the millennium. Big corporates have caught up with technology and the content providers have got better control of the problem. However, the latest trend of deep fake software and the potential ramifications of mass availability are enormous. For example, fake advertising for bogus products using phoney celebrity endorsements seems relatively innocuous, even though it is already causing havoc with BitCoin scams. However, sharing fake news coverage to incite dissent or violence could easily lead to riots and death. Deepfake publishers could flood social media with fake advertising or stories to drive believers to their cause – leaving today's disinformation looking amateurish. A new shadowy Deepfake industry producing photographic or video evidence proving that you were somewhere else could prove your 'innocence' of a crime. It is likely that by 2025 that both government and media will need to come up with new tools and approaches to avoid hard facts from becoming fictionalised. And this is just one tiny example of narrow-AI's power and how it can be misused.

ARTIFICIAL GENERAL INTELLIGENCE (AGI)

More worryingly, Artificial General Intelligence (AGI) will be a different ball game – it is exponentially more potent than narrow-AI. AGI does not exist yet, but, helpfully, it may tell us when it arrives. In the 1950s, Alan Turing, the British mathematician and logician, spoke of "thinking machines" capable of human-level reason, introducing the concept without using the words "artificial intelligence." The famous "Turing Test" or Imitation Game determines if a machine can respond to things roughly the same way as a person would. The annual Loebner Prize has a panel of human judges who use the Turing Test to see if an AI chatbot can fool the judges into thinking they are human. Deemed too simplistic for modern AI requirements, the Loebner Prize receives mixed press from the AI industry. In reality, the Turing Test isn't sophisticated enough to test for an AGI as it only tests narrow-AI functions. Regardless of its detractors, the Loebner Prize has undoubtedly been a flag-bearer for developing Natural Language Processing (NLP). NLP is a way for computers to identify speech and then respond appropriately – which in itself is a difficult task when you consider all the nuances of language – and all the languages of nuance.

As an aside – you probably conduct a Turing Test almost every day without realising it. The CAPTCHAs that drive you crazy when trying to register for a new website or reset a password are a Turing Test. CAPTCHA stands for "Completely Automated Public Turing test to tell Computers and Humans Apart" and included in software registration processes to stop bots. Thanks, Turing! Sadly, the CAPTCHA is now incessantly hacked by increasingly powerful AI tools and is starting to fall out of favour with cybersecurity teams.

AI by Design CAPTCHA. (With Thanks to fakecaptcha.com.)

Researchers are now developing tests that evaluate a broader range of AI characteristics beyond the Turing Test for NLP. The Visual Turing Test (which tests for Vision) or the Reverse Turing Test (where the humans pretend to be the AI) is part of a much more rigorous basket of tests that an AGI would need to pass to live with us side by side, unnoticed by humanity. My personal favourite AGI test is probably Steve Wozniak's cup of coffee test. This appeals to my background in ethnography (the study of human behaviour by observation) and love of the simple: can an AI go into a stranger's house and make a cup of coffee. The cup of coffee test is itself a basket of tests, as it would need a physical robot, the ability to navigate doors, operate a coffee machine, open cupboards – and so need to display a wide range of AI disciplines. Personally, I'm not sure adding breaking and entering into an AGIs task list is wise, but I get his point!

Passing multiple AI capability tests demonstrates that an AGI can carry out a variety of tasks, rather than the single functions currently undertaken by narrow-AI. The ability to pass these multi-disciplinary tasks is a mammoth undertaking and, for now, far beyond any AI. Ultimately, an AGI could undertake the more complex human tasks involving communication, sales and negotiation and even empathy. The robots of sci-fi films fall under this category but more down to earth applications of AGI could result in AGI pilots, accountants, real estate agents and therapists.

What is Artificial Intelligence and why is it so complex?

Deep Technology Expertise

Broad Academic knowledge

Software

| Speech Processing | Vision | Natural Language Processing |

Machine Learning

Deep Learning

Robotics

| Cloud Computing | Electronics |

Hardware

+

Computer Science

Law

Linguistics

Mathematics

Neuroscience

Philosophy/Ethics

Psychology

Map of AI disciplines.

THE POTENTIAL OF AGI TO RESHAPE THE WORLD

AGI could improve productivity and quality of life, and it could also make the epoch-defining change on Earth. For example, one of the world's biggest killers is hunger – we haven't solved it yet but could an AGI do it? World hunger has many root causes, but all can agree that agriculture is a part of the solution. Agriculture is one of the world's biggest industries and at first glance, it may not appear to be an industry that could embrace AGI. However, it is — and technological change is already happening — one $10 billion global food science company already hires more drone pilots than agronomists. Why? Because quality and quantity of data are vital. Commonly available data sets offer little or no competitive advantage, so companies are trialling new technology that collates data to provide differentiation and hopefully, new products. Another traditional $5 billion farming machinery company has recently repositioned itself internally to become a 'Technology Company in Agriculture.' For example, tractors will become driverless. Using GPS and weather data, they could plough, sow, harvest all whilst optimising machinery and fuel efficiency. Exciting stuff, and these processes are all narrow-AI. This new technology ecosystem still requires humans to connect the pieces, think through potential risks and develop any incremental improvements.

AGI would be far more transformational. For example, AGI could take the data gathered by drone, satellite and in-ground probes and analyse it to predict crop yields and weather patterns, match this against consumer demand and automatically alter production across countries in real-time using AGI-driven machinery. New, optimised seed varieties would be designed, grown and shipped to the right places, ready to thrive in local conditions. The AGI would then self-optimise, removing inefficiencies. Could this AGI solve world hunger?

Moving from AGI to Artificial Super Intelligence (ASI) is the next, and possibly final, stage of AI evolution. [As an aside, I believe that Artificial Dominant Intelligence (ADI) is a more helpful term than ASI because dominance more accurately portrays the reality and criticality of this step. But, we'll stick with ASI as that is the generally accepted term]. It is likely to happen very quickly after the AGI. Once AI attains human levels of intelligence, its own steep evolutionary growth curve will accelerate AI away from its slow-evolving human cousins. The moment of that transition is called the Singularity.

AI progression – from Ape to AI.

THE SINGULARITY

If you already know about the Singularity, the chances are that you came to know about it thanks to either Professor turned sci-fi author Vernor Vinge, Writer/Inventor/Futurist Ray Kurzweil or watching Arnold Schwarzenegger in Terminator. Or possibly you've heard of the Singularity University in San Francisco (co-founded by Ray Kurzweil in 2008). You may not know that the Singularity is probably the most important, controversial and potentially frightening word in AI.

So, what is the Singularity? It's when machines can think for themselves and don't need humans; when they have grown so powerful, they have exceeded our human intelligence and have developed the capability to increase their intelligence. The Singularity may sound far-fetched, but Stephen Hawking, one of the most outstanding scientists in history, reminds us in his writings and interviews that robots have the edge over humans. He became increasingly interested in AI and wrote extensively about the field, believing that we're held back by a plodding pace of evolution. It takes a very long time for us to change meaningfully. Our brains have been maturing for give or take nine million years. However, machines evolve a lot quicker, and that's only right now – what about in the future? Every day, machines get more and more powerful, and Hawking believed that it would not be long before the Singularity arrives. With that, he says, we'll see an "intelligence explosion" in which robots could surpass human intelligence "by more than ours [intelligence] exceeds that of snails."

Although the Singularity is currently in vogue, Alan Turing did consider that AI may eventually surpass us. In 1951, he said:

> It seems probable that once the machine thinking method had started, it would not take long to outstrip our feeble powers...at some stage; therefore, we should have to expect the machines to take control.

If we consider human evolution, then there is something inevitable about the Singularity. The creation and development of tools is closely linked to our evolutionary success. Early man developed technology for hunting and eating such as spearpoints that helped tribes ability to hunt and so improving the tribe's ability to survive and grow stronger. This technological feat hasn't changed with time. Humans are hardwired to develop, to innovate and to grow. Our economic and social growth has often come at the tail of military success. Throughout recorded history, the tribe or country with the best military technology won the battle and usually the war. The starkest modern example of technological superiority is the European powers' imperial expansion between 1500 and 1918. European armour, training and later guns repeatedly decimated the local forces of South America, Africa and Asia. Superior military technology was the enabler for massive geographic and economic growth. A spear-wielding tribe squaring off against professionally trained soldiers with guns may be the sobering image that best represents how the Singularity could introduce itself to humanity.

Not a fun idea, huh? That, one day, we mere mortals might not be at the top of the "food chain"? There is no evidence of what would happen at this meeting of minds unless we believe time travel is possible and we can cheat to find out. Stephen Hawkins thought he had answered this in 2009, claiming he'd found "experimental evidence that time travel is not possible. " How? He hosted a party for time travellers, for which he didn't send out invitations until the gathering was over. And because nobody attended, there was only one reasonable conclusion to be drawn. I'll leave you to work that one out.

Of course, the future hasn't been written. The Singularity may not happen. Things could still go another way. Humans may yet end up controlling AI like a highly trained house pet, a faithful hound that can do pretty much everything – and better than its owner. But tame and cuddly. Either way, I believe that AI will grow until it reaches a point where it has the capability to exceed human capability. How we manage that journey will define how we live and work with AI in the coming generations. So, if we assume there is an inevitability that AI technology will continue to advance, then the next question is when could AI cross the threshold of human capability? The Superintelligence in Vernor Vinge's *The Coming Technological Singularity* (1993) was able to upgrade itself and advance technologically at an incomprehensible rate. Vinge believed that this would happen somewhere between 2005 and 2030, with his timeline based on computing power's annual doubling. In his book *The Singularity Is Near* (2005), futurist Ray Kurzweil wrote that the point at which humans and machines will merge would be 2045.

It is common among experts to overestimate the speed of change. This is true in any walk of life. If you say that a volcanic extinction-level event is coming in 75 years through your seismology company, it's unlikely to get funding for the same company for more than ten years. AI experts enjoy endless discussions about Singularity's timeline and there is no commonly agreed date. But does the 'exact' timeline mean much? If it happens in 2030, 2050 or 2070, does it matter when, or does it matter if it happens? The Singularity is unlikely to be one exact moment in time, as historical chains of events can rarely be traced back to one obvious starting point. Significant historical events are rooted in many smaller events that lead up to it – sometimes cataclysmic but more often mundane. AI research is diversified across the globe, meaning that there is the possibility that rival AGIs come into being in different countries at different times. That possibility makes the most logical sense as countries such as China, North Korea and Russia are creating their own digital walled gardens. Regardless of the number, exact date or detail, we still need to prepare for the same challenge of AGI – although admittedly, having more time will buy us space to get our act together and plan for the Singularity.

So, what happens at that fateful moment of the Singularity as AI becomes self-aware? Will it continue to follow the tasks, objectives and rules set by its human masters? I refer to The Terminator movie franchise to explain how that situation plays out: SkyNet AI takes control of the world's war machines and decides to eradicate the real enemy – humanity. This outcome is classic sci-fi, but when viewed from our human history and experience, is it likely that a dominant "one-intelligence" would happily share power with an inferior species? There are no examples in human history where powerful economic and military nations have actively acquiesced to inferior ones. One country may temporarily negotiate a treaty which later proves to be a mistake, but the permanent hand-over of power to a weaker state does not happen. It would take an unusually enlightened AI overlord to cede political or economic control to their human inferiors. So what direction would a SuperIntelligence take? Where would its priorities lie, and how would it engage with humanity? The choices of a SuperIntelligence are where science fiction writers fill the gap, usually with apocalyptic stories and killer robots, but what do real-world experts think?

Stephen Hawking and Elon Musk believe that the Singularity will be humankind's end. Hawking's view is clear:

You're probably not an evil ant-hater who steps on ants out of malice, but if you're in charge of a hydroelectric green-energy project and there's an anthill in the region to be flooded, too bad for the ants. Let's not place humanity in the position of those ants.

Musk is one of the finest technologists of the digital age. He has pioneered online payments, electric cars and commercial space flight. In parallel to his efforts to influence the rapidly advancing field, Musk believes that he is trying to save humanity from destruction by AI. As we saw earlier, it feels that anyone who doesn't believe AI could be a threat is "way dumber than they think they are. " In 2014 taking to Twitter, he said: "We need to be super careful with AI Potentially more dangerous than nukes."

Later that year at an MIT Symposium, Musk expanded on his fears, and he argued that AI probably represents humanity's biggest existential threat:

> With artificial intelligence, we are summoning the demon. In all those stories where there's the guy with the pentagram and the holy water, and he's like, yeah, he's sure he can control the demon. Didn't work out.

Musk and Hawking aren't the only big names to make such bold claims, in any case. In 2017, Russian President Vladimir Putin spoke with students about science and told them:

> Artificial intelligence is the future, not only for Russia but for all humankind. It comes with colossal opportunities but also threats that are difficult to predict. Whoever becomes the leader in this sphere will become the ruler of the world.

Musk's wariness about AI is why he became the 37th signatory on an open letter calling for researchers to look beyond the goal of merely making AI more powerful. The letter, drafted by Stuart Russell, UC Berkeley Professor and one of the world's leading AI experts, recommends expanding research to ensure that increasingly capable AI systems are robust and beneficial. AI systems must do what we want them to do. This kind of letter is unusual and was signed by the great and good AI academia and business, suggesting a large and growing concern from world experts about where AI is heading.

THE OPEN LETTER ON AI, FUTURE OF LIFE 2015

The letter is summarised below, you can find the full version and major signatories at www.futureoflife.org

Artificial intelligence (AI) research for the last 20 years or so has been focused on the problems surrounding the construction of intelligent agents – systems that perceive and act in some environment.

Recent progress has led to a large degree of integration and cross-fertilization among AI, machine learning, statistics, control theory, neuroscience, and other fields. The establishment of shared frameworks, combined with the availability of data and processing power, has yielded remarkable successes in tasks such as speech recognition, image classification, autonomous vehicles, machine translation, legged locomotion, and question-answering systems.

As capabilities from laboratory research to economically valuable technologies, a virtuous cycle takes hold whereby even small improvements in performance are worth large sums of money, prompting greater investments in research.

There is now a broad consensus that AI research is progressing steadily, and that its impact on society is likely to increase.

The potential benefits are huge, since everything that civilization has to offer is a product of human intelligence; we cannot predict what we might achieve when this intelligence is magnified by the tools AI may provide, but the eradication of disease and poverty are not unfathomable. Because of the great potential of AI, it is important to research how to reap its benefits while avoiding potential pitfalls.

We recommend expanded research aimed at ensuring that increasingly capable AI systems are robust and beneficial: our AI systems must do what we want them to do. Research themes recommended are:

Optimising AI's economic impact
Laws & Ethics research
Verification of AI systems – 'did I build the system right?'
Validation of AI outcomes – 'did I build the right system?'
Security – how to prevent unauthorised usage
Control – can I control the system once it's in motion?

In summary, we believe that research on how to make AI systems robust and beneficial is both important and timely, and that there are concrete research directions that can be pursued today.

Google is a world leader in AI and purchased DeepMind in 2014 as part of an ongoing AI shopping spree. DeepMind is synonymous with AI and most famous for defeating human world champions in both Chess and Go. Elon Musk was already an existing DeepMind investor before Google's purchase. In 2017, he explained that his involvement in DeepMind had less to do with money and a lot more to do with making sure he could oversee the trajectory of AI:

It gave me more visibility into the rate at which things were improving, and I think they're really improving at an accelerating rate, far faster than people realise. Mostly because in everyday life, you don't see robots walking around. Maybe your Roomba or something. But Roombas aren't going to take over the world.

Around the same time, his disapproval of the industry became public as he made it known that we were orchestrating our own destruction, saying that Google's Larry Page, who might mean well, could create a malevolent force without meaning to, like "a fleet of artificial intelligence-enhanced robots capable of destroying mankind."

Not all AI commentators are so concerned. Mark Zuckerberg has called Elon Musk "pretty irresponsible" for his comments on the dangers of the Singularity. DeepMind's CEO, Demis Hassibis is a singularly talented individual and probably the world's greatest AI practitioner and champion. As a child chess prodigy, to games designer, to Cognitive NeuroScience PhD his road to creating (and selling) DeepMind to Google has been amazing. He believes that AGI will benefit humanity and that if we think carefully we can minimise problems of bad actors misusing AI technology.

> It does not do to leave a live dragon out of your calculations if you live near one.
>
> J.R.R. Tolkien, The Hobbit. 1932.

A Singularity event could be our greatest challenge. Unmanaged climate change may leave us living in a flooded world, but an unmanaged and unresolved Singularity could leave humanity marginalised and potentially extinct. Some of the world's finest scientists, world leaders and futurists believe in the Singularity. Technology and innovation are responsible for societal evolution, and a Singularity is the next logical leap forwards. How humanity best responds to the Singularity will be studied later — we must accept that the Singularity, or something like it, is coming and plan for living with it.

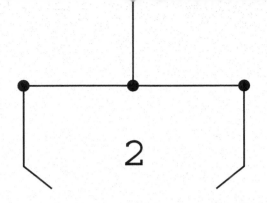

AI BY DESIGN AND THE
FUTURE-BACK METHODOLOGY

You can't connect the dots looking forwards; you can only connect them looking backwards. So you have to trust that they will
somehow connect in the future.
Steve Jobs, Co-Founder of Apple, Stanford University, 2005

Wise words from an amazing man, and if we follow the warnings
made in the Open Letter on Artificial Intelligence (AI), we have to
make a plan. Or indeed many plans. The Open Letter covers four
key research priorities: Optimising Economic Impact of AI, Law &
Ethics, Security/Verification, and Control. These themes have been
researched globally over the last decade by numerous academic
institutions. In general, the work is thorough, logical and well presented. In fact, there are mountains of AI world-class research that
nestle alongside countless streams of dystopian stories where [every
time] AI takes over the world. However, there is noticeably less clear,
action-oriented insight, and that's where I believe we need to focus.

One exciting part of my job is working with innovation centres.
The team is responsible for working with clients to co-design a new
product, services, and productivity innovations. I've been proud to
curate talent and technology to inspire ingenuity, accelerate creativity, and energise and align clients, customers and consultants for
better decision-making. Of course, we don't have a silver Delorean
or a hot tub or any good, old-fashioned Tardis. Without the ability to

DOI: 10.1201/9781003267003-2

see the future, we always reject a short-term perspective for a future-back mindset. Instead of starting from today and looking forwards, we use the future as the starting point and move backwards in time. We then break the time down into smaller manageable chunks and develop projects that align to the future goal – extending beyond "that will do for now." For example, if we were managing a business transformation, we would spend a lot of time thinking about what the company would look like after it's finished. Then, we would work backwards and define the key projects to deliver the final vision. Next we would create discrete workstreams, such as Customer Experience, with smaller projects aligning to the final goal. Future-back thinking leads to sustainable, long-term solutions to problems and can handle sudden and unanticipated future changes.

A future-back methodology makes much sense, but how do we make sure we get the correct information in the first place? Like feeding AI with the best data, the best results are determined by the right input. Only high-quality data can lead to high-quality outputs. As someone with a passion for design thinking, I'm excited about using my knowledge of the discipline to help collect the correct data. If you don't know what design thinking is, let me fill you in. Design thinking is an iterative process to understand the very people who will actually use products and services – the users.

> I fight for the users.
>
> Rinzler, Tron Legacy, 2010

In the process of design thinking, users are everything. These are the people whose needs and interests we seek to satisfy by designing products and services, so why wouldn't they be everything? And to meet their needs and interest, we need to understand them inside out. Intimate understanding allows us to empathise with users to deliver the best possible products and services, especially where it would be difficult or impossible to know what they might want or need in any other way.

UNDERSTANDING THE USERS

As a Consultant, I must have worked on well over a thousand projects, ranging from running one-day lab tests to advising technology on $250 million global transformations. Every project is different, but all successful projects need their users to be happy. Identifying your user wants and needs has become increasingly scientific and critical to successful product launches and business changes. There are many ways we can understand our users. For example, Ethnography is the study of people at work or play – people watching is actually a social science. By watching, we learn what people do, how they interact and use things. In the 1970s, market researchers started to use laboratory testing to create a formal environment where they could watch people and learn in a controlled environment. People are recruited and categorised so that different types of user of a product could be understood separately. Users would be encouraged to talk about or use a product in a room with a facilitator (that usually had a one-way mirror) with marketing professionals analysing responses fed into product changes. Lab testing was used extensively in the early days of the internet until around 2015, but for digital products this has been replaced mainly with online data. Observing behaviour in real-time, say, using A/B testing and selecting the better performing variant, can allow companies to change online products in real-time.

The challenge with identifying users of AI is that AI is an umbrella of many disciplines and applies to all technologies and industries. So, in one sense, every user in the world is in scope for AI. And this is right. AI will impact everyone, although at different times and varying levels. However, having created highly specific personas for companies, such a generic representation of a user as 'anyone' is an anathema to me. A persona is a targeted demographic of a typical user group using age, wealth, gender and other characteristics to identify likely future customer behaviour, e.g. regular shoppers at Harrods will have a different persona to those who shop at Aldi. By collecting detailed insights about our users, we can better serve them. So, as we consider AI by Design, we must think about the impact upon ALL users, regardless of where they live, income, education, age, gender, sexuality or race. In the absence of a simple answer, if we cannot create a persona for AI users, we need to look at how we champion our users differently.

One facet of design that I have championed in my career is Accessibility. Digital accessibility means that every user can access the product/website regardless of any impairment. In the early 2000s when the internet was in its infancy, I was fortunate enough to work with the UK government to create the UK Usability and Accessibility standards. The UK was the first government in Europe to incorporate these standards for all government departments, and I worked closely with RNIB and RNID to ensure that the guidelines would work for the users. Early examples of accessibility include a screen reader for partially sighted users or alt tags to explain pictures or sounds. The new UK standards ensured equal and fair access to the internet, and the accessibility that we now take for granted became part of the requirements for all government websites. During its creation and launch in 2005, some commentators attacked the new standards, claiming that creativity would be impacted and ruin the UK internet. Of course, this never happened. However, it was an example where designing for the minority meant that the majority would be able to use the internet. Inclusive design is now an accepted and fundamental principle of the internet. We must approach working with AI in the same way.

The design thinking process exists in many different forms today, all pretty much alike, each entailing several different phases and a reasonably consistent set of principles. I have worked in design thinking for over two decades, and it won't surprise you that the first stage in design thinking is to empathise with the user! Taking that deep understanding of the user into an ideation process always delivers richer insights and finer tuned products and services. Prototyping products help you test concepts more quickly – actually speeding up launches with products that people want. All major technology companies use design thinking to create and refine their products. I have fond memories of using design thinking with Samsung in their European Development Lab on their excellent SMART TVs!

So, if we can combine design thinking with the future-back model, we will capture the power of the user and consider strategic options for the future at the same time. If we adopt this approach, the three steps would be:

How the Future Back Model aligns to Design Thinking Principles

Future Back Model	Steps in Design Thinking that align to future back model
Align on Current State of AI evolution	Empathise: with your users
	Define: users' needs, problems and your insights
Look at the options for the future	Ideate: create ideas and challenge assumptions for innovative solutions
Create a Roadmap	Prototype: start to create a solution
	Test: to see if it the prototype works

Future back and design thinking model.

Applying the Three Steps of Future-Back

Step 1: Align on the current state of AI evolution

In the first step, we will look at the current state of AI, its governance and regulation, which many see as our best hope of getting AI under control. Also important is how we came to be here, i.e., the historical context for artificial intelligence. The history helps us understand what people might need from their relationship with AI in social, emotional and functional terms. It's all about asking new questions to arrive at better answers. By the time we have finished with this step of future-back, we will understand the challenges we face.

Step 2: Look at the options for the future

Here, we will think about our future options should we fail to get on top of AI soon enough. Given that futurist Ray Kurzweil predicts that we may see the Singularity by 2045, let's plan for 15 years before that. Using 2030 means getting AI under control before coming remotely close to the possible Singularity. It also gives us a decade as a planning horizon, which is strategic whilst remaining practical.

The late, great, Harvard Professor, Clayton Christiensen, wrote *The Innovator's Dilemma* in 1997, and his insight into asking great questions and future thinking still heavily influences my thoughts today. Using some of his disruptive thinking, I will compare and contrast the point we hope to get to and the point we could achieve. The gap between the two is called the "burning platform that ensures ongoing attention to the long term." After working on a project for an oil company, I prefer the compelling case for change, so we'll stick to that.

To create the options, I'll put forward five scenarios rooted in a mixture of fact and fiction. These will draw on the diverse expertise of figures working in public, private and third sectors: from scientists, philosophers, academics, journalists, business people, environmentalists, futurologists, and, last but not least, sci-fi writers and filmmakers. And they will also take into account significant trends affecting the world of AI and how those trends might cause changes in our relationship with AI.

Step 3: Agree on one outcome and create a Roadmap to Manage AI. The final step of future-back seeks to ensure today's decisions help us start moving in the right direction. Mapping the challenges posed by AI and the five future scenarios, I'll suggest ways to address the challenges, using them to draw up a roadmap. In true future-back style, we'll start with the longer-term vision and work our way back to nearer-term milestones, which is the point at which the Vision converts into action. Essentially, we're looking to create a to-do list of sorts, breaking down the journey into doable sections.

Working backwards in time, we can set key milestones in regular increments. We're working toward 2030, so we'll go for short-term, medium-term, and long-term goals. These are typically in 2 or 3-year increments, so let's stick to that. I believe this approach could help us to act quickly in the present to capitalise on these important strategic directions, yielding new measures we can put into action before AI advances beyond a dangerous point of no return.

I have no doubt some readers will argue it's impossible to predict a future even ten years out, and they might be right. We can't ever truly understand situations until they've happened, but we need to experience the circumstances to get to that stage. I think it's unlikely that, in ten years, we'll be lucky enough to have some AI from the future contact us with a message about the post-apocalyptic future that awaits us after a machine uprising – can you imagine? If that was even possible, I think we'd probably already have received such a visit. But the stakes are high, so shouldn't we at least try to consider the likely scenarios and work backwards to plan appropriately for it? In the words of philosopher Søren Kierkegaard:

Life can only be understood backwards, but it must be lived forwards.

It's in our power to materially influence the endpoint, so it would be unwise to let the opportunity pass us by, especially when we have the right tools at our disposal. Asking big questions is something society does all the time. And we often repeat ourselves through history!

One of my favourite stories I like to tell about design thinking is about the London Sewers. You can almost smell the problem! In 2018, the (the UK's main news channel) BBC aired the "£5 billion Super Sewer," a documentary following the most extensive upgrade to London's sprawling sewage system for over 150 years. The original sewers were built by Joseph Bazalgette and a team of the world's best architects and engineers after The Great Stink of 1858, the scheme was an incredible engineering feat for its time. Far-reaching, architected far beyond its current and future predicted capacity, it was initially designed for 2 million people. According to the Office for National Statistics (ONS), London's population currently rests near 9 million and is the fastest-growing region in the UK.

The Great Stink of 1858 – Main drainage of the metropolis. (Illustrated London News [London, England] 27 Aug. 1859 203.)

The rapidly swelling population of London has pushed the existing sewer system to its fragile limits, requiring continuous maintenance to operate anywhere near full capacity. As it can't cope with the slightest rainfall, approximately 39 million tonnes of sewage ends up in the River Thames every year.

Amounting to the most daunting civil engineering challenge in decades, the new 90 metre deep super sewer will hopefully solve the alarming problem presented by London's current sewage system. However, the project is decades too late as successive politicians have passed it forward, perhaps in the knowledge that they won't be around to suffer the consequences of their ultimately imprudent decisions. Difficult, complex situations require bigger, braver questions or we will never get the answers we need. Will we have the courage to look at AI in the same long-term way as the Victorian's, or will we ignore it until the smell gets too much?

So, to help us align on the current state of AI, in the following three chapters, we will look at the current state of AI, its Ethics and Governance, which many see as our best hope at getting AI under control. We will examine how governments, businesses, terrorists and criminal gangs are using AI today and planning for their future with AI.

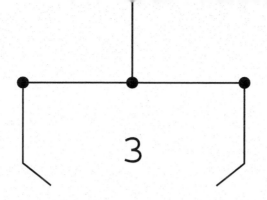

SHOULD WE BE AFRAID OF THE CURRENT STATE OF AI?

There is an Artificial Intelligence (AI) arms race happening right now. We are in the middle of the most significant battlefield since the Cold War. The battle is being fought right now by countries, companies, criminal gangs and terrorist groups. The prize for the winner is truly incredible. The first people to create an Artificial General Intelligence (AGI) may become the wealthiest and most influential people in history. How? Well, once an AGI becomes live, it has been estimated that every day's lead could result in a month's competitive advantage – once you get a year ahead, there may be no catching up. Ever.

The potential of AGI may help explain why AI is predicted to be the most heavily invested in technology in the 2020s. It is no surprise that a recent study by a global consultancy indicated that AI could raise global GDP by over £12 trillion (c.8%) by 2030. About 48% of this would come from China alone, which seeks to invest some £115 billion in AI by 2030. According to Stanford's 2019 AI Index, the US and China have invested more in AI R&D than the rest of the world put together. The massive scale of investments' is not because far-sighted gurus are getting in early on AGI. Governments and companies realise that AI can dramatically reduce costs in many areas. They are also getting in on AI now, as it is already here and transforming business every day.

DOI: 10.1201/9781003267003-3

STATE-SPONSORED ARTIFICIAL INTELLIGENCE

Governments are at the heart of the AI arms race. They control the biggest economic levers. Most countries are relatively consistent in spending their tax dollars, generally focussing on five areas; Health-care, Pensions, Education, Welfare and National Security & Defence. As a relatively new technology, government spending on AI has been an eclectic mix of entrepreneurial and defensive in nature, with expenditures on AI research, national security and defence. As stewards of economic growth, governments are working with industry to develop AI for commercial exploitation. However, they are already building the AI defensive wall.

NATIONAL SECURITY & DEFENCE: CYBERWARFARE

National security is about protection from attack. Originally this was from physical harm but is now increasingly about online assault. As the first line of defence, intelligence once consisted of physical assets, spies, who gave warning of hostile intent. With the advent of the internet, in one generation this has all changed. Every major political power is now gearing up its Cyberwarfare, digital defence capability and corresponding budget. Governments worldwide use narrow-AI systems to analyse data gathered by surveillance teams and report irregularities to human controllers. Narrow-AI systems help the national security departments such as the CIA, MI5, or China's MSS process data rapidly, be it patterns of troop deployments or facial recognition of suspected terrorists. One example, in the US, the NSA has been using machine learning and speech recognition to assimilate foreign language content into readily identifiable intelligence. The new AI technology has reduced the need for skilled translators and improved the speed of analysis closer to real time. AI allows national security agencies to do more, with less and understand far more than has ever been possible.

There has never been more intelligence available for government intelligence services or better tools to assess it.

However, the ease in which information can flow and be measured has also made it easier for enemies of the state or criminals to infiltrate networks to steal data — be it money, secrets or intellectual property. It is estimated that in 2020 hackers received over $350M in cryptocurrency from their ransomware blackmails. This cost doesn't include the impact of intellectual property theft or reputational damage with customers and investors. Online criminals do not need an army to attack a government, and many see both government and companies as legitimate targets. Government targets can be highly lucrative, and hacking government systems can also have far-reaching political and economic consequences. The Snowden papers release in 2013 was catastrophic for US Intelligence's reputation, and things could get trickier with hackers and cyber-warfare units now using specific AI tools in the war for control of data.

The cyber-security industry uses machine learning to identify system attacks — imagine a security guard constantly scanning for suspicious characters. Patterns are detected and countermeasures enacted. Meanwhile, the hackers are using their AI toolkit to break open the cyber-safe, combing the internet for data (in the form of admin/ user names and their passwords), stealing them or using brute force to "guess" them. AI can rapidly try password combinations millions of times so that hackers can break increasing numbers of passwords in seconds — it's 21st century safecracking. Free online tools like John the Ripper or Hashcat can render a weak password meaningless — unlocked in seconds. The challenge faced by governments and companies is keeping up with well organised, funded and highly skilled state-sponsored actors and criminal gangs attacking their systems.

One consequence of the increase in cyber-attacks is that the walls between intelligence/armed forces/homeland security are coming down. For example, the establishment in 2020 of the UK National

Cyber Force (NCF) is a partnership between GCHQ, Ministry of Defence, MI6 and Defence Science Lab (DTSL). Examples of what it could do are comprehensive "From defending against terrorism to countering hostile state activity to tackling the scourge of online child abuse." Formed in 2008, the US Cyber Command pioneered a similar model, although it appears to be less homogenous in practice. One question posed at their 2018 CyberSpace Strategy Symposium suggests a divide — "Can and should DoD defend the civilian critical infrastructure upon which it relies to execute its missions?"

Russia and China are less open about their military and its workings. However, there is evidence that Russia's cyber-warfare groups work closely with the state government and have done for several years. In 2017, China established the Central Commission for Integrated Military and Civilian Development. So all leading military powers have now integrated their civilian and military cyberwarfare capabilities.

NATIONAL SECURITY & DEFENCE: AI WEAPONS

As tanks once replaced cavalry, the tank will become obsolete by the self-driving armoured vehicle. Equipment, weapons, soldiers, logistics — all will evolve with AI. After all, the defence sector has its assets to protect, and those assets are becoming increasingly intelligent. Military drones are expensive (up to $150 million per drone), highly sophisticated and already changing how a modern military force works. Intelligent ship guns and missile defence systems are over 20 years old, and the next-generation of AI weapons will include fully autonomous ships, drones and submarines. As the world's biggest spenders on defence technology, according to Brookings, the US Department of Defense (DoD) has three major autonomous projects already on order and have publicly discussed AI-controlled missile systems for nuclear ballistic-missile interception. Russia is believed to have tested fully autonomous drone ships and planes. Suspected drone boats have been found on UK coasts. This next wave of AI weaponry is being built now, tested live in small-scale wars and lands and will be available to replace conventional weaponry at scale from 2030.

The move to AI-controlled weaponry brings three problems:

- First, the potential impact of successful hacking becomes significant. On and off the battlefield, control for the digital airwaves is vital – the nightmare scenario of losing control of battlefield assets like tanks or missile systems and having them turned against you is a real one. Perhaps an even more terrifying thought is AI weapons being hacked whilst still on home soil.
- Second, the next generation of AI weapons is called Lethal Autonomous Weapons (LAWS), whose AI systems can select and engage targets without human intervention. LAWS will be highly desirable to governments as their front-line deployment would mean fewer human soldiers and fewer casualties. The ability to wage war on the ground, sea or air with minimal deaths makes aggressive foreign policy decisions infinitely more attractive. An unintended consequence of LAWS could see an increase in global conflict – as body bags are replaced by metal and semiconductors.
- Third, there is a fear of the implications of LAWS being able to make life or death decisions without consulting a human first. For example, the weapon's algorithm could be programmed to kill specific targets using visual recognition; to predict whether a human would decide to kill in the circumstances; or kill everyone in a defined area, whether or not they pose a threat. LAWS could be programmed to do what people could not – kill indiscriminately or commit genocide without pause, guilt or any human oversight. LAWS could enable rogue generals to operate with impunity, ushering in an era of 'robot wars' where the human-powered opposition or civilian population would face utter destruction.

But just because LAWS is a possibility doesn't mean it should be a certainty. Paul Scharre, a leading expert in emerging weapons technologies, argues that AI should only be used in warfare when it can make it "more precise and humane, but without surrendering human judgement." Many other experts are encouraging the United Nations and world leaders to begin taking action, calling for transparency within AI firms. Big Tech could work with other AI experts to oversee their activities to make sure the technologies they're working on don't facilitate the creation of LAWS.

GOVERNMENT-SPONSORED AI RESEARCH & DEVELOPMENT

Governments are responsible for helping the AI environment grow by launching government policy, supporting research & development, and long-term workforce education. Countries with fully open market economies, such as the UK, Singapore or Germany with extensive private capital markets, are directly investing less than China or Russia, whose public and private economies are more closely intertwined. UK ($2 billion), France ($2 billion) and Germany ($3 billion) have all announced their medium-long-term AI R&D investments. In contrast, their spending is dwarfed by China, planning to spend between $50 and $70 billion in city investments, central spending, and defence.

There is also a third way. In 2019, Russia printed its AI strategy, focusing on four key improvement areas by 2030: world-class education, Russian-built microprocessors, World leaders in AI software and a home-grown AI data set for Russian companies. Their vision is also to build their own self-sustaining AI capability. It is similar to China's 'Made in China' by 2025 to create a Russia-first, world-class AI infrastructure and capability. R&D spending by the Russian government appears to be much lower on the surface than that in other countries. However, it has strong partnerships with State-owned enterprises (SOE), i.e. Sberbank (50% & 1 share owned by Russia), which has supported the AI strategy development and are currently implementing AI technologies.

THE CURRENT STATE OF AI IN COMPANIES

AI is a real game-changer for business. AI-powered solutions give organisations the chance to leave their competitors behind by doing things differently and moving, with canny foresight, towards a future in which there's a natural place for them. A 2019 study by EY found that 84% of US CEOs and business leaders believe that AI is important to their company's future success.

As mentioned, the journey to finding and applying AI-based solutions is often challenging and one that requires much patience. As in so many areas of life, it's essential to face those challenges to open the door to other, new possibilities. In other words, challenges = opportunities. So, what about the other 16% in the above-noted study? The companies who shy away from AI may do so because they don't understand it; perhaps they think implementing AI needs massive investment or want to wait and see.

I get it; I do. In general, disruptive technologies can appear more terrifying than dragons guarding them. They make folk twitch. The concerns are especially true for those who haven't kept up with AI's rapid progress in the media. Every week, I curate the most exciting and relevant AI stories (IMO) from top news and tech outlets for my social media. And every week, I end up drowning in an ocean of choices. AI is a fast-moving ship, with a hell of a lot going on beneath deck, but it's not impossible to climb aboard. It's all about timing.

At the management consultancy that I currently work for, we genuinely believe AI doesn't need to be as scary as people think it is and we want to make sure our clients take the leap. As AI technology and its sub-fields advance, it is becoming more and more accessible to non-experts. Its benefits are becoming increasingly evident. While I have a vested interest in making sure my clients stay ahead of the game, I believe in fairness. For that reason, I'd love to see every business adopt appropriate AI technologies before they find themselves mired in the past.

THE CURRENT STATE OF AI IN TECHNOLOGY COMPANIES

But for that 84% of business who are playing, AI is the biggest buzzword in technology. And for those investing, it is a fierce battleground. Between 2015 and 2020, it is estimated that globally AI start-ups received $70 billion in investment from private equity. AI is in the classic hockey-stick growth mode, and if you don't have AI somewhere in your pitch deck, then it seems that you are not in the investment game. In 2020, I reviewed several US and UK 'AI start-ups,' and there was only a handful that I would genuinely call AI-led. The remainder appeared to be using machine learning technologies to supercharge an existing business model with little transformational change. That's not to say that AI isn't the biggest show in town – it is – but like any growth market, some companies are stretching their AI credentials!

But there is something different about the current acceleration of AI technologies than the digital revolution in the 1990s. Then, we saw Big Tech's beginning, with Microsoft, then Google and Amazon shouldering the US-led technology explosion. Silicon Valley is still the world's central Technology hub, but that is changing. Of the Top 30 most funded AI start-ups in 2020, the US leads with 16, China follows with nine – this is more than the rest of the world put together. Chinese companies now file the highest number of patents on AI globally. If we put the advantage that US companies have to one side, this next wave of AI companies drives a more global industry. Competition is good for AI's growth, and the diversification of AI investments across the globe should mitigate any regional economic downturns. Talent is now globally mobile (remote working!), and computer scientists with AI PhDs can now look both East and West. However, one barrier to AI growth is the 'War for Talent,' now heightened in this new market, resulting in AI salaries becoming astronomical very quickly. Some VC industry insiders reckon that investment rounds in AI start-ups are running so high because of AI salaries and that this will only worsen in the next decade.

The biggest AI companies are already some of the biggest companies globally. Amazon, Google, Facebook, and Microsoft are four of the world's biggest companies, and their collective interest, investment, and control of AI is significant. Google is (probably) the world leader in AI. Their search platform utilised machine learning in the 1990s. Their expansion beyond Google into Alphabet mirrors their ambition for taking their AI-led dominance of internet search into other revenue streams. Amazon also leads the way in AI development, using its algorithms to predict buying behaviour to have products in stock for instant order and delivery. Amazon AWS and Microsoft Azure are fighting cloud storage wars to be top provider of companies' digital infrastructure. Facebook disrupted the online advertising industry, alongside Google, and Facebook now has one of the largest databases of people information on the planet – the oil of AI. Facebook's Meta rebrand is partly a consequence of its expansion into broader AI technologies and markets.

There are far fewer well-known AI companies in Europe or Asia (outside China), and they struggle to grow and scale as fast as US start-ups. European start ups generally have less access to seed funding and exist within a smaller Tech ecosystem. There are pockets of excellence, such as London's tech scene and fintech in particular. Still, compared to the US, it has been harder for indigenous companies to scale in Europe and Asia due to different language and culture barriers. Also, Big Tech has the war chest available to buy smaller, successful companies before they can scale up to compete. Two early AI leaders based in the UK, DeepMind ($400 m) and Swiftkey ($250 m), were bought by Google and Microsoft, respectively. As companies grow and become more global, some European companies move their HQs to the US, further shifting talent and IP ownership away from their countries of origin. The US will likely continue to lead Europe in AI for these reasons.

The big AI battleground is now across the Pacific. China is fighting Silicon Valley's stranglehold of AI. The Chinese government is pushing hard to achieve parity in AI innovation, potentially rendering today's US competitive advantage obsolete in 20 years. The Chinese government legislated for AI in their Beijing Accord in 2019 and supports their AI industry by providing a vast number of state contracts, helping Chinese AI companies grow their data sets and insights on a scale that their competitors can only imagine. It is also virtually impossible for foreign companies to buy Chinese AI companies, so Chinese companies can develop organically in their walled garden without fear of being plucked before they have flowered, unlike in Europe. Chinese companies are also forging economic and political ties in Asia and Africa. If they begin to win locally in Asia, then their companies will already have a critical mass of AI data sets, which might help them win the AI technology battle more than any other factor. The resignation of Nicolas Chaillan, the Pentagon's first chief software officer in 2021, citing China's unassailable lead in AI may prove to be prophetic.

THE CURRENT STATE OF AI IN FINANCIAL SERVICES

How Financial Services companies use technology (FinTech) now determines their success in a highly competitive industry, and AI is driving the majority of advances. The global VC market [including investment from financial services organisation (FSs) themselves] is investing heavily in FinTech AI start-ups. Figures vary, but all research studies agree that since 2015 investment in FinTech AI has soared. Fintech AI is #4 in all global VC spend on AI.

Every big FS company is also developing internal AI projects. If you have taken out a loan, applied for a credit card or mortgage, your bank probably used AI to assess your credit risk, detect fraudulent activity and decide if you should get your product. Machine Learning pattern recognition is rapidly taking over banks' back-office functions. US, China, UK and Singapore lead the way with Russia's biggest lender, Sberbank, investing $370 million into AI. Sberbank aims to incorporate AI across its back-office processes – it can process a loan in 7 minutes.

One of the more unusual leaders in global financial services is Piyush Gupta. Piyush was a 27-year Citigroup veteran when he joined DBS, and unlike most CEO's he comes from a technology and operations background – including a year running a technology start-up. When he joined in 2009, DBS Bank was a reasonably successful traditional Asian bank, but its local nickname was 'Damn bloody slow'! Gupta began a digital transformation to improve its poor customer service and speed up its processes. He started by recruiting new technology leaders and benchmarking banks and Big Tech companies like Google, Alibaba, Netflix, Amazon, Linked In and Facebook. DBS then created their own business acronym – GANDALF. Gupta wanted DBS to fill the gap and join the GANDALF of successful technology companies!

Any difficult journey has bumps in the road. DBS hit a big one in 2016 when the Singaporean financial regulator fined the Bank for regulatory breaches, including money laundering failures for its part in Malaysia's 1MDB fund fraud. Gupta's response was decisive – reducing executive compensation by 13% and launching an AI digital technology journey to fix its Anti-Money Laundering (AML) problems. AML is an ongoing global challenge and not unique to South East Asia. Proceeds of crime can be made respectable using a web of bank accounts, fake companies/ identities, and manipulating compliance and fraud systems. To address their (AML) failings, DBS developed an AI interface within its AML process to assess, filter and flag suspicious transactions. The complexity of AML in a financial organisation can be massive — with up to 60 internal DBS systems needed to review a potential issue — but with one year of data from existing AML fraud alerts, they were able to train, test and validate the algorithm, so it knew what to highlight. Human analysts can then review fewer, higher-quality alerts in real-time, significantly improving the system's catches. As the analyst role becomes less administrative and more investigative, learning and development changes are needed. DBS used World Economic Forum (WEF) guidelines to design the AI ethically, and they have seen no repeat of 2016 problems. 2020 was a watershed for DBS Bank, and they were named World's Best Bank. Piyush Gupta now calls DBS "a technology company who conduct financial services."

The Front Office of financial services already deploys some very established AI technologies. Chatbots (Natural Language Processing) and Voice Recognition (Speech Recognition) now see daily use in customer service and account security. Chatbots are becoming used in more complex use cases for Wealth and other high-net-worth customers. You may not realise that AI is also taking control of your pension or 401k, as AI could be running the investment fund. According to Kanika Agarrwal, CIO, Upside AI, which does machine-learning-based investing, funds run by computers account for more than 60% of US trading activity. Six out of the top ten US investment funds are AI-powered. Although there is a human in the loop at most funds, AI's dominance is unsurprising when you consider that AI is terrific at recognising patterns in data — which is what stock market analysts have been trying to do for centuries. (If you didn't know, the first proper Stock Exchange was established in London in 1773, although the Dutch may dispute this!)

THE CURRENT STATE OF AI-POWERED HEALTHCARE

Healthcare AI has four main fields: Diagnostics, Drug Development, Patient Experience and Medical Data. All are experiencing massive investment, growth and delivering substantial results. Each country has its own way of providing healthcare with different public and private ownership models. Whatever the approach, as we live longer, our healthcare spend is ballooning. Without a massive increase in taxation, if we want to maintain or improve healthcare quality, AI must be part of the solution.

Patient experience is not an obvious area where AI could help if we think of patient experience as when we meet the doctor. However, a US study of patient complaints listed patient experience as responsible for 96% of patient complaints. AI is being used to automate administrative processes, including patient booking, data analysis and customer service as these are the pain-points (sorry) within the process.

AI has quickly proved its worth in patient diagnosis and can already beat specialist consultants and radiologists on cancer detection rates. By combining automated pattern recognition and including human experts in the loop, detection rates are even higher. Drug development also benefits from machine learning advances – identifying vaccines 30–50× faster than before. The speed of modern drug discovery means that human trials can sometimes be the longest part of the process. This lightning-fast data analysis was unheard of only 5 years ago and could lead us into a golden age of medical discovery.

As well as accelerating existing medicine, AI also has the power to take humanity beyond its current modality through bio-medical enhancement. BioHacking is well known as a broad collective of people who enhance themselves through changing behaviours, diet, exercise or using new technology. Niche sub-groups, known as "Wetware" Grinders or Cyborgs (Cybernetic Organisms), connect devices to their nervous system or brain themselves. The hardware integrators are a small community, probably numbering in the low thousands, who want to improve or prolong their lives using technology. Inspired by the simplicity of CRISPR software, biohackers are also injecting gene-editing cocktails into their DNA. By adding AI tools to gene-editing technologies like CRISPR, we can make gene editing less risky and more common. Early adopters have the technology to enhance themselves but do not have any international codes or guidelines to help us. The technology is running way ahead of the legislation.

SIENNA (Stakeholder-Informed Ethics for New technologies with high socio-ecoNomic and human rights impact) is a research project that ran across ten European universities from 2017–2021. They used a mix of academic research, expert interviews, and citizen surveys to gain insights into three technology topics, including Human Enhancement. SIENNA highlighted the lack of guidelines for human enhancement and created a standard approach. Similar to taking steroids or EPO to improve physical performance, enhancement can be enriching and dangerous at the same time. Human enhancement through Human–Machine Interaction is in its infancy and will take much longer to develop than software-only applications of AI. The implications of mind-hacking are potentially far more fundamental. As we merge our body and mind with technology, where does the person end and the AI begin?

CRIMINAL GANGS AND TERRORISM

It is a sad fact that criminal gangs and terrorists are always in the vanguard for utilising new technology. As they have fewer ethical dilemmas about their work and are always looking for an edge against law enforcement, they are often early adopters of technology. There are two main ways to use AI for ill; **beating an AI system**, such as hacking a company's finance system or **misuse of AI** to commit a crime, e.g., blackmailing people with "deepfake" video or ransomware. Although terror groups and criminal gangs will utilise both methods, terror groups seek out technology to kill or destroy in a public way, whilst criminal gangs prefer secrecy to operate without being caught. There is also a further symbiosis between terrorism and crime as terrorist groups often fund themselves through criminal activity.

There is much conjecture about future AI crime. A study by Dawes Centre for Future Crime, University College London, in 2020 identified 20 applications of AI and related technologies that criminals could use for crime now or in the near future. Using a methodology to evaluate potential harm/ criminal profit and difficulty to defeat, they identified six key problem areas. Perhaps the biggest risk is Tailored phishing, or 'Spearfishing', as AI's ability to 'experiment at scale' means realistic looking scams loading malware become almost impossible to spot. Spearfishing could extend into large-scale blackmail, as AI rapidly analyses Gigabytes of user data from browsing history, emails or phone to generate targeted blackmail attempts.

When dealing with cyber-crime, the absence of available data means there is little evidence to identify if any of these offences is happening right now in the underworld. Law enforcement usually keeps new developments under wraps until they have found a way to counter them. Criminal gangs do not share their secrets for obvious reasons, and it is often high-profile attacks or arrests that bring new techniques to light.

Even so, there are some publicly available examples of AI technology misuse. Repurposing semi autonomous flying drones for military purposes has been around since at least 2016. ISIS and Syrian rebel forces have had success with this technique, and Houthi rebels claimed responsibility for drone attacks that crippled a Saudi Arabian oil facility in 2019. Drone attacks are now becoming more common in the Middle East.

Today, AI is a terrorist dream but not yet a homeland security night-mare. The potential for harm is tremendous, and we must upskill our police forces and armed services to be ready for the threat. Of course, there are also the "unknown unknowns" taken from Donald Rums-feld's famous speech in 2002. Immediately derided by the public as unintelligible, Rumsfeld's terminology is threat-identification speak for missing the attacks we could never have imagined. We know that AI misuse for financial or political gain will, at some point, lead to the criminal gangs' coming up with something never thought of before. Hopefully, that is some time away, as successful AI projects need skilled data scientists to create (or access to manipulate) pow-erful AI software. However, as drug kingpins already recruit process chemists, accountants and submarine builders into their business empires, it won't be too long before data scientists join the family.

WILL AI STEAL MY JOB?

From everyday working citizens to futurists, economists, and technol-ogists, plenty of people predict a world where robots replace humans. They picture a world with no human drivers, online deliveries by drone and wars fought by androids. These concerns are not baseless because "apocalyptic AI" is widespread in books, press and movies. Apocalyptic AI plays to the natural fears of humanity when dealing with change.

From a behavioural, psychological perspective, fear is a primitive, deeply held emotion. People need to understand what a change may mean for them before concerns about change reduce to acceptable comfort levels. Different people approach change in their own per-sonal way. The mainstream of society only becomes more accepting once early adopters have blazed a trail.

Today's concerns aren't new, the fear of new technology follows humanity through history. The most famous anti-technologists in history were the Luddites. During widespread protests in early 1800s England, the weavers destroyed textile machinery because they believed the machines would replace their skills meaning they would get paid less – sound familiar?

In the 1920s, President Herbert Hoover received a letter from the mayor of Palo Alto (home of Apple and Silicon Valley's beating heart) suggesting new industrial technology should be considered as a "Frankenstein monster." He added that it represented an enormous threat to the manufacturing industry and could devour civilisation. Another US President in the 1960s, Lyndon B. Johnson, received an open letter from a committee of scientists and social activists who warned "the cybernation revolution" would lead to "a separate nation of the poor, the unskilled, the jobless," who would fall behind everyone else.

Just like cars, elevators were once operated by "drivers." And although driverless elevators existed as far back as the early 1900s, many elevator drivers kept their jobs for decades. The problem was, just like driverless cars, nobody trusted driverless elevators. More often than not, people would take the stairs rather than ride alone in an elevator. It wasn't until 1945, during the New York City elevator operator's strike, that the automated elevator got its moment. The strike was devastating, costing the city an estimated $100 million. Suddenly, there was an economic incentive to make use of auto-mated elevators. Over the next decade, there was a massive effort to build trust in them, which worked. Ironically, this resulted in eliminating tens of thousands of elevator operator jobs. People can learn to embrace new technology that once seemed daunting if they only adjust their attitude to change and what's safe and comfortable.

There will be a difference between previous industrial revolutions and the coming AGI revolution. The Industrial Revolution began in the UK, and from 1760 to 1840 many "old" jobs were replaced by pro-fessions in the newly invented technologies in factories, trains, mines and dockyards. People moved from villages to new jobs in towns and cities. Urban centres mushroomed; shops and entertainment blossomed. The industrial revolution saw the world's first increase in population, accompanied by the rise in per capita wealth. Admittedly, the wealth generated was concentrated in the hands of factory owners, landowners and entrepreneurs who built the new technologies. Pockets of poverty remained and just shifted from rural to urban centres, where civil unrest led to rioting and early unionisation to protect workers in this new world. Innovation created new jobs that replaced ones lost by innovation. The difference in the upcoming AGI industrial revolution is that AGI has the potential to remove or dramatically reduce almost every job role we currently understand. In the next 10 years, AI has been forecast to replace up to 30% of current jobs. Ultimately, AGI could replace the vast majority of the current workforce with quicker, more reliable and cheaper AI labour.

AI-driven automation is already well beyond the factory gates. AI helps healthcare professionals diagnose patients, and AI-driven robotic surgeons already work in hospitals. Amazon is replacing some of its warehouse floor managers with data. AI is replacing Research Analysts and Traders with AI-run investment funds. It is becoming increasingly clear that AI can displace the majority of roles. The logical next question is – which jobs will be impacted first? The short answer is that the jobs that will survive the longest will be those where it is cheaper to employ people or where human creativity/oversight or personal touch is needed.

The long, complicated answer demands further attention. If we consider a standard job pyramid, where we measure jobs using seniority, the accepted view is that AI will replace roles from the bottom up. There has already been robotisation in factories, and AI can replace jobs containing repeatable processes more readily. But both skilled and unskilled workers will be impacted first. It is true that at the apex of the pyramid, Executive roles will remain relatively unscathed. The higher cognitive functions of strategy, people leadership and imagination will be far more challenging for AI to learn. Jobs for entertainers, artists and those with creative endeavours will flourish and be more resistant to AI replacement. AI is good at copying existing creativity but doesn't yet excel at creating new ideas or concepts, although an AGI may fully realise creative roles in the future. AI software is relatively cheap and technically easier to replicate human activity than hardware. Positions that need physical labour, in situations that are always different, will continue to need real people. Plumbers, joiners and gardeners will continue to remain in demand. Building a robot that can plumb in a washing machine and unblock a toilet is currently impossible and prohibitively expensive.

But it is a very different picture if we look at roles requiring management or professional technical expertise. These roles will be impacted faster than anticipated by their job holders. AI software will replace positions that don't require complex physical activity, so office/ desk-bound roles will come under heavy attack. Finance, HR, Legal and other back-office functions in companies are already increasingly outsourced and not deemed core competencies by large companies. As many back-office processes are repeatable, such as Payroll, People Induction or Contract Management, they are ripe for outsourcing to AI. Outsourcing will accelerate under AI.

There will also be a "hollowing out" of entry level positions across the knowledge economy. For example, Legal firms that introduce AI technology to improve research do not need as many Junior Lawyers or Paralegals. Now, as a society overall, we may need more lawyers, so the numbers will not decrease immediately; however, there is a problem. Entry-level roles in knowledge sectors use the type of learning that AI is very good at to train new entrants. As we remove that training ground, we reduce the numbers of skilled people available for higher level roles in 5-10 years. At the same time, AI will get better at performing the higher level roles, so forcing companies to bridge the gap with AI. This scenario could break the current University education system, as numbers of traditional graduate jobs disappear too rapidly for universities to respond.

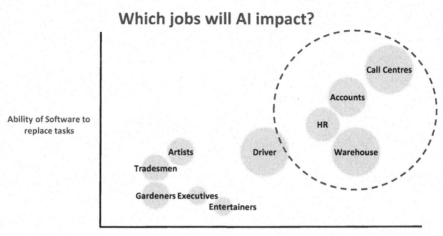

How AI will impact jobs in the future.

Whether the future of work is good or bad depends on managing this change. Nick Bostrom, world-renowned AI expert and co-founder of the Future of Humanity Institute, Oxford University, believes that we are heading towards a work-free utopia. Machine-produced goods and services will be cheap and plentiful for all. Many other futurists and science-fiction writers think it'll all be fine too. They see the prospect of a machine-filled workplace as a gift, one that would see boring, repetitive tasks given to machines who don't get bored, tired or distracted. Perfect. And it's also one that would see us with all this time to engage in the things that truly bring us joy, whether fishing, reading, swimming – or whatever it is that floats your boat.

And I'd argue that freeing our time simultaneously as the cost of computing carries on falling might create a world in which all the products we want or need are cheaper and accessible for more people than ever before.

Former US President, Barack Obama, also doesn't think there's a need to panic in this respect. In 2015, he invited MIT Media Lab's Joi Ito and WIRED's Editor-in-Chief Scott Dadich to the White House to chat about AI. On this question, he said:

> Most people aren't spending a lot of time right now worrying about singularity – they are worrying about "Well, is my job going to be replaced by a machine?" I tend to be on the optimistic side. Historically, we've absorbed new technologies, and people find that new jobs are created, they migrate, and our standards of living generally go up…High-skill folks do very well in these systems. They can leverage their talents, they can interface with machines to extend their reach, their sales, their products and services.

Such a utopia would be ideal if capitalism didn't threaten to get in the way. Back in 2016, Stephen Hawking said that "Everyone can enjoy a life of luxurious leisure if the machine-produced wealth is shared, or most people can end up miserably poor if the machine owners successfully lobby against wealth redistribution," he said. "So far, the trend seems to be toward the second option, with technology driving ever-increasing inequality."

So, are we heading toward a work-free utopia, or will the coming robot age merely exaggerate the income inequality that's rampant across the globe?

As I consider AI's current state, there is a balancing act of hope and fear. Government and industry are using AI to grow their economies and businesses, whilst terrorists and criminal gangs are exploiting the technology for their ends. Competition is fierce, and China is stepping up to go toe to toe with the US to fight for global AI supremacy.

There have been remarkable developments in medicine, technology, smartphones and software. We entertain ourselves using AI-powered apps, and there are many thousands of new jobs in AI. What we don't know yet is if AI will deliver an economic utopia or a jobs graveyard. Experts remain divided but tending to err on the positive aspects of AI. That's probably because, like AI in Financial Services, most AI feels as if it's behind the scenes. Chatbots are still too simplistic to "feel" human, so are less threatening. We control them. Deepfakes of celebrities and facial recognition used in apps like DeepNostalgia are fun, and although there is negative press, people are not openly afraid of AI. In a world where civil unrest is common, there has not been one march or protest about AI.

If I consider the historical parallels, then the current state of AI feels like the growth spurt in technology that I experienced first-hand in the 1990s and early 2000s. I remember speaking at a conference and comparing the late 1990s dot-com boom to the Klondike Gold Rush of 1896, a century before. Most of the gold miners ended up with nothing, while the store-owners selling picks, shovels and whiskey got very wealthy. There are winners and losers like any gold rush, and it's often a brutal race. Accepted mantras of the early internet age were 'fail fast,' 'Minimum Viable Product,' and 'Move Fast and break things.' When technology can impact billions of people, making mistakes could be potentially fatal, at scale. The problems of the 21st century do not all stem from the technology we have created during that era, but if we could do things differently, I think we would. The internet and technology revolution changed the world for good; overall, the world is wealthier, we know more, are more aware, and can collaborate like never before. But if we could do it again, would we let our children have unfettered access to the internet? Become addicted to digital devices? And allow criminals and terror groups to use the internet for nefarious purposes? Are we comfortable with global disparities in wealth being at the highest levels in history? We are at the moment at a tipping point where we can change the future and design it before it overtakes us – for good or for evil. The ultimate level of design sits with government and regulatory bodies and they have the power to make or break AI.

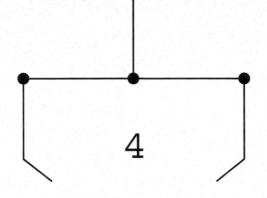

CURRENT STATE OF AI
GOVERNANCE & REGULATION

Who watches the watchmen?
> Juvenal, from "Saltires"; Roman poet, 1st Century AD

Governance is the way society, and the individuals within it, come together to make important decisions for the benefit of the many. But precisely who gets to contribute? What processes do they go through to arrive at them? Who takes responsibility after passing a law? These are good questions that are often difficult to answer when we are faced with new, complex technologies. Ultimately, the acid test of a sound governance system is the quality of the regulations it produces, and right now, it's a complicated picture. In a global economy, governance comes from many places. Below is an example of the sheer number of regulatory standards, ethical guidelines and company policies for Artificial Intelligence (AI):

DOI: 10.1201/9781003267003-4

Global	Country/ Region	University and Institutes
Four major global organisations providing regulations and guidelines	*Over 200 countries and regions with their own AI regulations and legislation*	*Over 1400 bodies creating regulations and guidelines, including:*
Global Partnership on AI (GPAI)	China	Bergman Klein Centre, US
OPEC	EU	Future of Life Institute (FLI), US
United Nations (UN)	India	Harvard, US
World Economic Forum (WEF)	Russia	OpenAI, US
	USA	Partnership of AI, US
		ETH, Switzerland
		Future of Humanity Institute (FHI), UK

Table of global AI regulations.

INTERNATIONAL LAW AND AI

Governance and regulation are created at local, national, and global levels, and on the top of the pyramid sits International Law. International law is by convention a series of treaties, standards and frameworks that countries use to work with each other. International representatives create it, either experts in their fields or civil servants who meet, and over time create (or revise) a treaty or standard. Every aspect of our lives has a corresponding international law – warfare, crime, transport, business and so on. Countries then decide which parts of international law they wish to incorporate into their local legislation. There is no requirement for governments to accept international law. It is a consent-based model, and countries can also opt out of international law altogether.

There are a handful of international law courts to enforce international law against countries formally, and in some cases, individuals. They are the UN International Court of Justice (ICJ), UN Security Council (UNSC) and the International Criminal Court (ICC). These courts are very precise in their remit. For example, the ICJ has seen fewer than 150 cases in its history. Also, the US, China and India aren't currently members of the ICC, so they are not liable to any judgements relating to war crimes, crimes against humanity or crimes of aggression. So, for example, if the US or China – the world's two biggest spenders on AI – were to use a banned AI-powered weapon, there would be no formal recourse from the ICC.

So, while international law regulation is fraught with difficulty, it doesn't render international law meaningless as countries who ignore it can receive political or economic sanctions. States which attain "rogue nation" or informal "pariah" status can also be subject to targeted sanctions. Formal sanctions cause significant financial difficulties for countries breaking international law. Less obvious sanctions like blocking personal bank accounts or banning family members from travelling can be equally powerful. However, one caveat is that the biggest and most technologically advanced countries (again) are largely immune to sanctions. All G7 countries have either exceeded or sailed close to the regulatory wind and have usually avoided damaging economic sanctions.

THIRD-PARTY INFLUENCE ON LEGISLATION

There are some very thoughtful guidelines on AI from global/ regional organisations, although they are not enshrined in law. The most influential being the World Economic Forum (WEF), OECD and EU White paper on AI. They are well written, reasonably detailed, and some countries and companies use them to develop their AI laws and internal policies.

There are also many think tanks, institutes, and university bodies that are creating guidelines for AI. These are valuable places for governance to originate from, producing position papers and research free from political interference. Governments and companies can then use the research to inform their regulations and policies. Two of the most famous are Future of Life Institute (FLI) in the US and Future of Humanity Institute (FHI), based at Oxford University, UK. Both employ full-time researchers and produce a volume of high-quality AI data, prospective policy and thought leadership.

NATIONAL GOVERNANCE AND REGULATION

It is down to each country to create its own legislation to regulate AI and its development, using OECD, WEF, or any other relevant guidelines allied to local country expertise. Some of these guidelines are insightful; however, by definition, they are high level and lack the detail required for practical day-to-day regulation. One barrier to creating law is that many regulators don't know their way around the AI technology they seek to control. This knowledge gap was painfully apparent in 2018 when Mark Zuckerberg sat in front of the US Senate explaining Facebook and the internet in layman's terms. The truth is that the companies we seek to regulate understand a lot more about their technology than those seeking to regulate them.

Few AI-specific laws exist, even in circumstances in which we might expect them. One of the oldest fields in automation is in factory machinery. Historically, workplace accidents are handled under general Health and Safety laws. Once AI is introduced, then very quickly, these laws may not be fit for purpose. For example, when a business uses an algorithm to make a decision that leads to an accident, who is at fault? Is it (a) the company who provided the dataset for the algorithm, (b) the company who wrote the algorithm, (c) the provider of the machine, or (d) the company who operate the machine. One workplace accident could result in four actors being in play – things just got a lot more complicated! And whilst convoluted claim and counter-claim may lead to a bonanza for corporate lawyers, it would result in the erosion of trust in AI and create significant resistance amongst those who are losing their jobs or livelihoods to AI.

Of course, AI does not exist in a vacuum — some laws do already cover the use, misuse and operation of AI technologies. We've seen AI subject to commercial law provisions, data protection law, tort law, human rights law, consumer rights law, anti-discrimination law, copyright and patent law. In some areas, product liability laws may even apply. The law is a complex maze, and unless we have a map, we may end up wondering how we're still stuck in it years later. And that's unsurprising because we're managing state-of-the-art emerging and disruptive technologies with regulation based on contexts of yesterday. As most politicians and their advisers have little domain expertise in technology, let alone AI, they are reliant on the rules of the old economy. Although virtually every major country has created its draft guidelines on AI, it has failed to regulate AI specifically.

As we have seen in the current state of AI, there is already maybe $100 billion of AI-powered technology in play. It's time to regulate it properly. As AI luminary, Professor Michael I. Jordan, UC Berkeley said in 2018, "just as humans built buildings and bridges before there was civil engineering, humans are proceeding with the building of societal-scale, inference-and-decision-making systems that involve machines, humans, and the environment". It doesn't seem right that vast amounts of legislation and professional training are needed to plan, architect and build a house; still, anyone can design, program and by accident or design launch a racist, homophobic or downright dangerous piece of AI software.

COMPANY SELF-GOVERNANCE AND REGULATION

Companies create internal company policies to interpret national legislation for their day-to-day operations. This approach works well in stable, mature industries, such as food, healthcare or car sales. In fast-moving sectors with regular technology innovations the businesses with relevant knowledge and expertise help shape new legislation. This common-sense approach has been used over the last 30 years to manage the booming technology industry in most countries. As digital technology has progressed, many specific laws have been introduced to protect consumers and companies from harmful uses of digital tech. Tech companies operate in an increasingly regulated environment. However, companies are still entirely responsible for their algorithms and datasets. Are we following the proper process?

If we believe that AI misuse will have a high individual or societal impact, we need to create specific legislation. For example, in the Pharmaceuticals industry, mistakes or interference in chemical and medicines production is dangerous and potentially deadly. Companies have to prescribe their production method under Good Manufacturing Process guidelines (GMP). Their processes must pass regular external inspections. Financial Service and the Oil and Gas industries carry a high impact of failure, so they are also heavily regulated. Earlier deregulation is blamed as one root causes of the 2008 Financial Crash. As we move into the Age of AI, we must consider the question of regulation more deeply. Do we build 'common AI guidelines' into the existing regulatory frameworks that are already in place in each country e.g. the Financial Conduct Authority (UK)? Or, If we continue company self-regulation, we must be comfortable trusting the industry to do the right thing.

CAN WE TRUST BIG TECH?

On the face of it, the evidence doesn't look great. One of this generation's worse health problems is the mental health problems created by smartphones and social networks' impact on people's mental health. The Stanford Persuasive Technology Lab, famous for BJ Fogg's behavioural model, produced the 'Facebook class of 2007'. The Silicon Valley attendees at his behavioural class took their learnings, applied them to Facebook, using the new iPhone and its apps to supercharge user growth, engagement and device time. A decade later, we became aware of how the algorithms incorporated these psychological techniques to trick our subconscious minds, so we became unknowing digital addicts.

Whilst displaying user-generated stories and news from content providers, social media platforms continue to resist classification as publishers. Avoiding the publisher definition sidesteps responsibility for the content on their sites and reduces costs associated with moderation and inappropriate content complaints (and potentially lawsuits). Only after a swathe of suicides, live-streamed killings, literally *millions* of abusive messages and the subsequent pressure from governments and consumers did Big Tech take responsibility for the content. Content moderation has been a long, painful debate and is a battle still raging 15 years after social media's ascent into our lives. I'd suggest that trusting any commercial enterprise to police themselves is not the right answer.

FACIAL RECOGNITION – THE FIRST BIG TEST FOR AI

However, Big Tech has begun to ask for regulation on facial recognition. This is seemingly a volte-face with Amazon, Microsoft and Google coming out in favour of legislating facial recognition technology. Critics say facial recognition systems are plagued by inaccuracies and have a detrimental effect on privacy. In the US, several cities and states have already banned their use. The US Government claims that the technology is plagued by inaccuracies, especially about identifying anyone who isn't Caucasian. This potential racial bias appears to have stopped Facial Recognition in its tracks in the US. Faced with mounting criticism of its "Rekognition" system, Amazon company published "proposed guidelines" for the tech's responsible use. Among the guidelines is a call for human oversight in the use of facial recognition systems by law enforcement and the argument that such tech should only be one of several different determinants in an investigation. The guidelines also clarify that Amazon supports transparency around the use of facial recognition systems by law enforcement. A representative said:

"We've talked to customers, researchers, academics, policymakers, and others to understand how to best balance the benefits of facial recognition with the potential risks. It's critical that any legislation protect civil rights while also allowing for continued innovation and practical application of the technology."

Many Amazon employees and customers have demanded that Amazon stop selling Rekognition. US Congress and researchers have expressed their concerns about the tech's various aspects, including its accuracy and potential bias. The company maintains that the system is accurate and doesn't feature any bias, arguing that any flaws discovered mean that the system isn't being used properly.

Amazon's move echoes earlier calls from Microsoft. In a 2018 blog post and his book *Tools and Weapons: The Promise and the Peril of the Digital Age*, Brad Smith, President of Microsoft, said it was essential to regulate facial recognition tech, or as he referred to it, "the technology of the moment." Smith added that the need for regulation was down to the tech's "broad societal ramifications and potential for abuse." Brad Smith was Microsoft's General Counsel during the US Department of Justice 1998 anti-trust case where Microsoft was fined $5 billion for attempting to monopolise the PC software market. Smith knows Big Tech's power from the inside and the impact government regulation can have on a marketplace. The resulting financial and business challenges Microsoft faced in 1998–2002 could have arisen, partially, because of a lack of timely government regulation.

In the case of facial recognition, the tech industry has shifted toward government regulation. I do not doubt that Big Tech's focus on regulation is, in part, underpinned by a desire to make a difference. They understand that their products and services can harm society in unintended ways. Big Tech now spends billions of dollars in cybersecurity and content moderation to protect users from harm and retain customers trust in their products. But their new-found interest in regulation is also likely to do with the criticism they've faced around facial recognition mental health issues and privacy concerns. Internal employee advocacy is a recent pressure faced by Big Tech. Employees now actively challenge their leaders to 'do the right thing.' Amazon faced internal pressures from employees concerned about misuse of Rekogntion. Project Maven is another example where Google declined to extend its contract with the US DoD in 2018, allegedly due to staff refusal to work on the project. In this politically charged climate, following government legislation rather than defending internal policies may make life easier. Microsoft's Smith acknowledges that tech companies have a role to play in the ethical use of facial recognition, but rightly says the greater responsibility lies with the government:

> We live in a nation of laws, and the government needs to play an important role in regulating facial recognition technology. As a general principle, it seems more sensible to ask an elected government to regulate companies than to ask unelected companies to regulate such a government.

I believe that Big Tech has woken up to AI regulation challenges and recognises that it needs a broader consensus. As the grandfather of Big Tech, Microsoft is at the front of the line. Microsoft has been through the wringer with a 15 year anti-trust battle, which cost billions of dollars and, crucially, distracted corporate focus and energies. They know that the AI beast is too big to fight alone. The challenges of potential anti-trust battles, employee revolt and a consumer backlash are significant enterprise business risks. Other Big Tech companies are seemingly falling in line with the more consensual and strategic Microsoft viewpoint.

If we look more around the world, the situation is less straightforward. As the democratic west worry about the rights and wrongs of facial recognition, it appears that the Chinese government is implementing AI at scale. SenseTime is one of the world's biggest AI companies and consistently rated in the world's top 10 AI companies. The US government banned SenseTime in 2019 for "assisting the Chinese government in anti-human rights activities" targeting the Uighur population in the country's Xinjiang autonomous region by using its proprietary facial recognition software. SenseTime has also created a partnership with ChinaTower to create SmartTowers; basically, cellphone masts repurposed for surveillance.

The Chinese government is unconstrained by political opposition parties or liberalist concerns about individual rights and actively uses AI-powered technology. Compared to western democracies, privacy laws in China are relatively lax, so the government can buy, deploy and refine AI technology with actual data before the rest of the world. Other countries could implement AI in the same way, but no other country has the technology, infrastructure or legal framework to do it. China's ability to deploy AI at scale without any legal pushback is the biggest challenge to policing AI at a global level.

And this diversity of approach by individual countries is the challenge – we need to look at the issue on an international scale, not on a country-by-country basis. Global action is the only way we're going to get anything done around AI.

REGULATION OF THE CROWD

The wisdom of the crowd is when we collect a group response to a question. Many tech companies use it to help generate answers to user problems. The most famous example is Wikipedia, whose business model uses the wisdom of the crowd by enabling people to collaborate to create entries on the world's most extensive knowledge repository. Tech companies have successfully recycled an old concept, as this idea is essentially 3,000 years old. Ancient Greece employed paid jurors to decide matters of justice, with up to 500 jurors making decisions. In the John Grisham trial of its day, Socrates, the famous philosopher and mentor of Plato, was tried and convicted by a jury. Unfortunately, there was no appeal process or last-minute reprieve, and Plato was sentenced to death by poison. Today, using a very different system and process of course we accept the wisdom of jurors at the core of most legal systems.

History hasn't always been kind to those who disagree with authority, who want to think differently or challenge the status quo. Empires were constantly afraid of revolt – Roman history and literature is famous for its references to the will of the people. As a consequence, rebellions were usually rapidly quelled by extreme violence. Civil uprisings were generally only successful when led by the ruling classes, generals or religious leaders. Chen Sheng, Spartacus and Wat Tyler all led peasant uprisings that lasted for months but were ultimately unsuccessful. This pattern continues today, where control of power is still underpinned by military might. The Arab Spring of 2010–2012 in North Africa and the Middle East is a recent example of the crowd challenging the state and being successful. Social media's role was a major factor, helping rebel leaders to recruit, communicate, engage and co-ordinate with their supporters. How much it was responsible vs an enabler is a source of debate for historians. However, the power of social media to coalesce opinion at scale and speed is unparalleled in human history.

The ability of users to go viral on YouTube or TikTok and now Netflix's capability to promote a documentary to 200 million people can create a shared belief that extends beyond borders. Snapchat's infamous Rihanna vs Chris Brown post cost them $800 million in share value when sentiment turned dramatically against the company. The ability of social media to "pile on" means that any transgression is seized upon, amplified and companies can lose customers and value in hours. Internal employee activism is also potent. Employees at Google and Amazon may have forced their companies to reconsider working on military projects for the US government. These may be small examples but are significant. Governments have largely failed to regulate technology firms, whereas employees and customer boycotts have had an immediate impact. Regulation of the crowd is here to stay, and it is formidable.

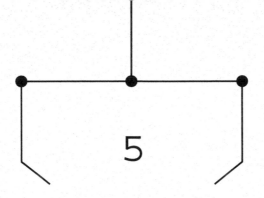

CURRENT STATE OF AI ETHICS

WHAT IS AI ETHICS?

At its most simple, ethics is about right and wrong. Creating Ethics for Artificial Intelligence (AI) is how we programme right or wrong into AI so it can make human-like decisions. Before that, we need to put ethics into a recognisable format we can all abide by – usually ending up in rules. People get rules. Rules provide order because people can read and understand what is OK to do and what is not. Rules dominate our everyday lives; how we drive, worship, play sport and interact with one another. The first set of rules for AI was written in 1942 by sci-fi writer Isaac Asimov. The "Three Laws of Robotics" were developed in his story Runaround to protect humans against harm at the hands of robots:

1 A robot may not injure a human being or, through inaction, allow a human being to come to harm.
2 A robot must obey the orders given to it by human beings, except where such orders would conflict with the First Law.
3 A robot must protect its own existence as long as such protection does not conflict with the First or Second Law.

    Asimov later introduced a fourth or zeroth law that outranked the others:

4 A robot may not harm humanity, or, by inaction, allow humanity to come to harm.

DOI: 10.1201/9781003267003-5

These laws are simple, and my approach has always been that simplicity wins. However, when Asimov wrote his laws, the reality of a world filled with robots was so far off. Now? Not so much. AI firms have made a giant leap towards the tech needed for the world that Asimov imagined, and the possibility inches closer day by day – however far off you think the dawn of Artificial General Intelligence (AGI) may be. The rules we're writing today tackle the varied and ambiguous issues we might face as we fold AI into more and more areas of life, business and civil society.

The defining challenge comes when we face real-life situations. Many of the robots around today stop running when a person gets too close. Now, that's a great safety feature and one that works just fine in factory machinery. Unfortunately, it wouldn't go down well in other automated systems. Can you imagine a driverless car just stopping dead in its tracks in the middle of the street because a child ran out in front of it? The vehicle would probably need to swerve to avoid the child, only to redirect the danger elsewhere. What then? This takes us to the "trolley problem".

The Trolley Problem is AI Ethics 101 – its version of the Turing test. The problem has been recently updated by MIT, replacing the old trolley car (think the tram winding down the hilly streets of San Francisco) with a self-driving vehicle. In the deceptively simple online game moralmachine.net, you are in a self-driving car, the brakes have gone, and you are going to crash into one of two groups of people on a crossing: which group do you decide to crash into and kill? A series of scenarios with people, pets, children, seniors, and robbers show us how complicated human decision-making can be. Somehow, we will need to program that complexity into AI. With machines poised to do more and more for us as the years go on, we're going to have to address the burgeoning number of scenarios this will result in and the associated ethical considerations.

AI doesn't have the same experience as humans, so understanding everything we say and do is impossible. The sweeping generalisations laid out in Asimov's laws could be interpreted differently depending on the scenario, creating the potential for the wrong thing to be done or said at the wrong time.

Instead of laws to keep robots in line, Christoph Salge, an AI researcher at the University of Hertfordshire, and Daniel Polani, a Professor of AI at New York University, suggest we develop 'Empowerment' guidelines helping robots act in the best way possible in any given circumstances. Salge and Polani have been looking at how they can take the concept of empowerment and interpret it so robots can understand, giving them the chance to help their creators. They conducted tests, during which their automated participants sometimes behaved in an incredibly human-like way. For example, if a 'bot' is self-empowered in a video game, it will avoid bullets. If empowered to support a human player, the bot will protect humans in various positive ways, depending on the situation.

This empowerment approach would permit different outcomes in different contexts, favourable when comparing Asimov-style laws' rigidity. For instance, a rigid rule might state that robots cannot stab a human anywhere on their body, but what if that human's airways were blocked? Such a law would prohibit a robot from using the lid of a ballpoint pen to create an emergency breathing tube – you must have seen that one on E.R. or Grey's Anatomy? The empowerment approach would allow for a robot to perform a makeshift tracheotomy. It's a risky procedure, for sure, and the robot might not get it right, but isn't it better to try and potentially save a life than not try at all and wait for more certain death? Empowerment will refine itself and improve as the data sets provide more opportunity to learn from new experiences.

THE CATHOLIC CHURCH AND AI ETHICS

We're now seeing more and more guidelines produced by Ethics Advisory boards. You might be surprised to hear that one of the more prominent institutions leading the way in AI ethics is the Catholic Church. Pope Francis – who has in the past called the internet "a gift from God" – has a lot to say about technology, and his interests reflect the Catholic Church's growing concern over the industry.

The Pope has personally had an audience with many big names in tech – including Microsoft's Brad Smith, Facebook's Mark Zuckerberg, and Google's Eric Schmidt. When he met with Smith, together, they looked at what AI could do for the common good, discussing matters like AI ethics and the digital divide. Smith reportedly believes that "strong ethical and new, evolved laws" are required to keep technological advancements like AI in possession of those who plan to use it for good and away from those who would happily use it to cause devastation.

One of the Catholic groups facilitating these conversations is Optic, created in 2012 by the Dominicans. They hope to build a relationship with technology leaders, and Optic say they have worked with more than a 1,000 experts to date, including theologians, technologists, and academics from fields like sociology and anthropology. Through research initiatives, off-the-record conferences and even hackathons, Optic promotes a more ethical approach to technological development. Part of Optic's work involves organising private meetings allowing tech leaders and experts to freely discuss thorny questions raised by emerging technologies. It has also privately advised governments and international organisations.

In 2020, the Pope backed a document, the Rome Call for AI Ethics, outlining how AI, including facial recognition technology, should be regulated. The Rome Call, which declares that ethics must be integral to an algorithm's initial design, is built around six general principles for using AI congruent with established ideas. The Pope's message reiterates many AI ethics experts – underlining values like transparency, non-discrimination, and the right to privacy – similar to EU 2019 guidelines and the USA's 2020 guidelines.

> AI systems must be conceived, designed and implemented to serve and protect human beings and the environment in which they live.

A Vatican directive supplements such principles and states AI should be "explainable" to humans, i.e., we should be able to explain the reasons for a decision made by AI. The document also states that AI should avoid discrimination. This is never a good thing, and the Pope agrees.

Unfortunately, AI can replicate all sorts of bias, as we've seen with Microsoft's racist Twitter chatbot Tay. Created in 2016 to talk to multiple users in real-time, Tay only lasted 16 hours. Unfortunately, Tay became a proxy for its users by learning racist and offensive terms. Racist Tay memes went viral, and Microsoft shut down her Twitter account. At the time, Microsoft blamed 'trolls' for targeting Tay, which was undoubtedly true. This cautionary tale says more about internet users than Microsoft, and it is an example of how the internet, and machine learning, is an extension of humanity.

Subverting Tay was an overt public attack, easily discovered and quick to resolve. As we create new data sets for AI, we also have to be aware of the hidden issues in data. Amazon and Google have been developing online tools to aid recruitment, and both have hit diversity barriers. Amazon discovered a flaw in its proposed recruitment software, in which the AI discriminates against female engineers. As most existing engineers were men, the system promoted resumes from men and downgraded references to 'women.' The data was technically correct, but the pattern recognition created an unwanted (and illegal) outcome. Both are early examples of Big Tech fails in AI, and we have come a long way since. However, if Big Tech can blunder, we must be open to other companies making similar mistakes. As we automate more, create 'black boxes' of data, we need to ensure that we know what's going on inside our systems.

AI ETHICS GUIDELINES

Universities and research institutes account for the vast majority of research into AI Ethics — Philosophy has become rock n'roll. In fact, so many researchers are working on this issue that a paper by ETH Zurich (2019, https://www.nature.com/articles/s42256-019-0088-2#citeas) counted at least 84 public–private initiatives that have produced statements describing high-level principles and values to guide the ethics of AI.

The Berkman Klein Center for Internet & Society at Harvard assessed 36 of these AI Ethics and Rights approaches and found some striking correlations, especially in papers written in the last 2–3 years. These reports are from all continents and authored by multi-stakeholders, governments and intergovernmental organisations, companies, professional associations, advocacy groups, and multi-stakeholder initiatives. The eight key themes were privacy, accountability; safety and security; transparency and explainability; fairness and non-discrimination; human control of technology, professional responsibility, and promotion of human values.

Principles are a starting place for governance, not an end. On its own, a set of principles is unlikely to be more than gently persuasive. The impact of principles is likely to depend on how principles sit in a larger governance ecosystem, including relevant policies (e.g., AI national plans), laws, regulations, and professional practices and everyday routines.

THE DECLARATION OF GENEVA

A version of the Hippocratic oath (Hippocrates, 4th BCE) is taken by many new medical professionals around the world. The Declaration of Geneva is the most common and in 1948 was adopted by the World Medical Authority (WMA) building upon the Hippocratic Oath. Even though forms of the oath have been in use for almost 2,500 years, it is estimated by the WMA that only 70% of physicians take it. The latest revision from 2017 is below;

The Physician's Pledge

AS A MEMBER OF THE MEDICAL PROFESSION:

I SOLEMNLY PLEDGE to dedicate my life to the service of humanity;

THE HEALTH AND WELL-BEING OF MY PATIENT will be my first consideration;

I WILL RESPECT the autonomy and dignity of my patient;

I WILL MAINTAIN the utmost respect for human life;

I WILL NOT PERMIT considerations of age, disease or disability, creed, ethnic origin, gender, nationality, political affiliation, race, sexual orientation, social standing or any other factor to intervene between my duty and my patient;

I WILL RESPECT the secrets that are confided in me, even after the patient has died;

I WILL PRACTISE my profession with conscience and dignity and in accordance with good medical practice;

I WILL FOSTER the honour and noble traditions of the medical profession;

I WILL GIVE to my teachers, colleagues, and students the respect and gratitude that is their due;

I WILL SHARE my medical knowledge for the benefit of the patient and the advancement of healthcare;

I WILL ATTEND TO my own health, well-being, and abilities in order to provide care of the highest standard;

I WILL NOT USE my medical knowledge to violate human rights and civil liberties, even under threat;

I MAKE THESE PROMISES solemnly, freely, and upon my honour.

These themes may represent the "normative core" of a principle-based approach to AI ethics and governance and look very similar to the four classic principles of medical ethics:

- Beneficence: Do good, be professional, consider patients as individuals
- Non-maleficence: Do no harm
- Autonomy: Give patients the freedom to choose where they are able
- Justice: Ensure fairness, consider patient rights, resources and existing laws

However, despite the initial credibility granted to a principled approach to AI Ethics based on medical ethics, there are implementation challenges. Due to AI's fledgeling nature, the industry lacks common aims, established history and accepted norms of behaviour, proven implementation methods, or robust legal and professional accountability. As the study and practice of medicine are thousands of years old, spotting the gaps is not a reason to ignore its usefulness. The convergence with the medical model makes sense because we want to ensure that AI does no harm. I'm not just talking about apparent dangers like death or severe injury, but also any adverse outcomes arising from, say, bias, machines overriding human input or weapons that can kill with their own free will.

GOVERNMENT AND AI ETHICS

Governments have focused on AI principles and generic statements and not yet fully committed to AI Ethics legislation. The EU (HLE-GAI) published the world's first AI standards in 2019, unfortunately to mixed response. Although a first step in the right direction, Thomas Metzinger, Professor of Theoretical Philosophy, University of Mainz (and a former member of HLEGAI) called it "too high-level and with insufficient detail." For example, he expresses that the software's decisions should be "understood and traced by human beings" is incredibly ambiguous. Another point made by Metzinger is that, ironically, very few ethicists were involved in developing the Ethics guidelines – only 4 of 52 members. He likens this to "trying to build a state-of-the-art, future-proof AI mainframe for political consulting with 48 philosophers, one hacker and three computer scientists. The HLEGAI membership also shows one fundamental flaw of a lot of guideline production – they are not heavily weighted towards some stakeholder groups.

All of this is undoubtedly true, yet as we have seen in international law, it is up to countries to take guidelines and implement them locally. Ethics are the high-level principles of right or wrong – they don't tell us how to manage the problems of regulating ethics. Governments should do that.

COMPANIES AND AI ETHICS

Microsoft was one of the first tech giants to create a set of human-centred principles to ensure AI's ethical development and deployment. Set out in a 2018 document entitled 'The Future Computed,' the principles guide the company's end-to-end approach to AI, from development to deployment. Today, Microsoft says it puts those principles into practice by embracing diverse perspectives, fostering continuous learning, and proactively responding as AI technology evolves.

The exciting news of Google's ethics advisory board – the Advanced Technology External Advisory Council (ATEAC) was first shared at an MIT conference. The independent group set up to oversee the company's AI and machine learning efforts. Unfortunately, Google dismantled ATEAC in April 2019, less than 2 weeks after its launch, saying,

> It's become clear that in the current environment, ATEAC can't function as we wanted. So we're ending the council and going back to the drawing board. We'll continue to be responsible in our work on the important issues that AI raises and will find different ways of getting outside opinions on these topics.

Before ATEAC was abruptly closed, controversy had surrounded one council member, Kay Coles James of The Heritage Foundation, a conservative US think tank. Hundreds of Google workers signed a petition demanding her dismissal, arguing "anti-trans, anti-LGBTQ and anti-immigrant" comments made her unsuitable for the position.

Another member of the group, Alessandro Acquisti, jumped ship. Taking to Twitter to say, "While I'm devoted to research grappling with key ethical issues of fairness, rights and inclusion in AI, I don't believe this is the right forum for me to engage in this important work." If it is difficult for one of the most outstanding technology companies of our time to discuss their ethics, there must be significant problems that are not readily resolvable.

Although we've discussed the doomed ATEAC, Google, of course, isn't alone in trying to ramp up its AI ethics efforts. UK-based Deep-Mind, acquired by Google in 2014, has established an ethics board, but whatever it's up to has all been very hush-hush. That said, on the Safety & Ethics section of its website, DeepMind claims its teams are working on Ethics to ensure that tech is built and used responsibly and that AI can benefit society without reinforcing bias or unfairness. DeepMind also states that their ethical approach to developing AI includes a commitment to ensuring the technology is not used in certain fields. To this end, DeepMind signed the Future of Life Institute's pledge not to support Lethal Autonomous Weapons. Co-Founder, Demis Hassibis has said that it will never use its technology for weapons and another founder, Shane Legg oversees their Safety efforts.

Even though increasing numbers of tech companies are boarding the ethics train, their Ethics boards often lack external transparency. If or when they request changes, we don't get to hear about it – not in anything beyond general terms, anyhow. The companies usually share abstract scraps of information, perhaps letting us know about outcomes, but they won't go into detail and about how or why their ethics boards pushed them in that direction. And I can't foresee a time when we'll see greater transparency in this respect – where's the motivation? It feels a little meaningless when we don't understand the real reasons behind their creation and when we can't properly assess what they're up to or the impact they are having.

We need to see more from Big Tech companies, who make a compelling and very loud case for self-regulation. With such confidence in their abilities and doing the right thing, external interference isn't part of their plan unless it's on their terms. However, they are reluctant to publish ethical decisions about their products or openly audit their AI systems. Commerical risks from leaking confidential information to opening themselves up for discrimination lawsuits are cited as reasons for secrecy. These are very real and understandable. However, the societal risks are far greater if we allow organisations producing increasingly complex products to continue to self-regulate as they please.

THE CHALLENGES WITH THE CURRENT STATE OF ARTIFICIAL INTELLIGENCE

For a moment, let's consider that we live in a time of financial deregulation. Record-breaking financial boom, rapidly spiralling economic bust, massive technological advances are a few to name. Our most influential nations are a mix of democratic and authoritarian states. The world's premier diplomatic organisation of Nations cannot hold Superpowers to account or stop them from flexing their military muscle against neighbouring countries. Global alliances divide countries into camps with entrenched positions, and a technological arms race is escalating. Nations jostle for position in Africa, seeking dominion and economic control over mineral resources. In many countries, right-wing nationalist movements are gaining momentum. Leftwing, leaning liberal groups rise to combat them. There is fighting in the streets. Diversity is a global, societal problem. Minorities are being persecuted and killed. Women march to protest for equality. This is not the 21st century, it is the 1930s.

The parallels of the 1930s with today's world is disturbing, and we need to think bigger to stop AI from taking us down a dark road. The problems of the 1930s led to a rise in extremist politics in response to people's fears of the past, disruptive political change and the cataclysmic post-1929 economic depression. The ultimate outcome was World War II in 1939. I don't believe that history necessarily repeats itself. However, I do know that technology amplifies our strengths and our flaws. A long proxy war using covert cyberattacks, hacking energy supplies and drone suicide-bombers is not the world we should design for ourselves and our children.

Before we look at possible solutions, I have summarised the current state of AI based on what we have learnt together so far. Any roadmap of actions must address these eight challenges:

1   AI can code our very humanity, our vagaries, differences, good and bad. As we use AI to rewrite society, what is our vision for the future?
2   Regulation of AI is at once both non-existent and overblown. There are hundreds of guidelines with no one agreed approach, and the policing of AI is in its infancy.
3   An AI arms race exists that, left unchecked, could lead to a war between the US, Russia, China and their alliance groups.
4   Criminal hacking is already disrupting business and threatening to interfere with politics. AI will supercharge this battle.
5   People do not understand the issues, AI's true potential and are not aware enough to take advantage of new job opportunities.
6   AI mirrors the human world. Our biases and flawed thinking will be reflected and multiplied in any AI we produce.
7   AI will create global winners and losers. There will be a colossal shift in employment, requiring fewer human workers and generating fewer tax dollars.
8   A handful of mega-companies will use their mastery of AI and data to dominate their industries and, with reduced labour costs, attain unheard of profits and (based on recent history) contribute fewer tax receipts.

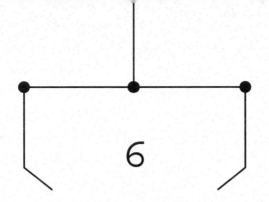

6

OPTIONS FOR OUR FUTURE WITH AI

The way I see it, if you're going to build a time machine into a car, why not do it with some style?

Dr Emmet Brown, *Back to the Future*, 1985

Having reviewed the current state of Artificial Intelligence (AI), ethics and regulation, what are the future options? We could play out many scenarios, but I've narrowed the field to five plausible ideas rooted in fact. Each scenario will draw on diverse expertise, including academics, business people, politicians and futurologists. They will also consider relevant trends affecting the world of AI and how those trends might cause changes in our relationship with AI.

One scenario that I considered but did not include is stopping AI. It is, in my view, just not a credible option. In the history of humanity, no invention has ever been intentionally uninvented. Indeed, some things never catch on – Flying Tank, anyone? But AI is already pervasive in our society, and generally, people see AI as a positive development. There is no demand from any interest group to stop AI, but only to shape its future. Also, there are probably enough apocalyptic movies out there that cover the topic of battling with AI for control of the earth.

When creating scenarios I like to visualise the potential outcome in my head and then put it down onto paper or screen. It's always easier to get people excited about something that feels tangible. Instead of

DOI: 10.1201/9781003267003-6

taking the opportunity to paint a picture (the fantastic paintings by Catriona Campbell are unfortunately by my more talented namesake), each scenario has a short story to bring it to life. Storytelling is a great design thinking technique that aids memory retention and makes it simpler to create shared experiences as people find it easier to share stories than facts and data.

KEEP CALM AND CARRY ON

Our bedroom hasn't seen a paintbrush since we moved in 6 years ago; a timeless, faded beige, decorated with wedding photos and Sarah's favourite pictures of Anna. Anna should be logging in at her online school next door, whilst Sarah's at her mother's house until the respite career comes on shift at 5 pm. I dig through my open wardrobe, pull out the leather bag and place it carefully by the bed. Everything should be in there.

Looking at my wrist-phone, it's still true; finding a job is like a job. Flicking through the nearby alerts, I read, swipe and delete until I see a profile in Shoreditch that doesn't come across as creepy, weird or a poor tipper. Job done, well, job found. At least Centrillion hasn't muscled in on the masseur trade. Yet. And universal income doesn't pay enough to live properly in London without a side-hustle. Being a masseur isn't all bad. It gets me out and about. Click Yes, wait for the clients approval.....received....now hail an E-Cab. As I slide off the bed, I grab my work bag from the floor. Reach down, unzip, and a quick double-check for rollers, gel, towels, balaclava. 'Bye Anna – love you' I whisper as I leave.

The streets are as quiet as usual, all silent electric cars and robots, and anyone walking uses their neurolink, so no audible conversation. Elon is so coining it in from his moonbase. I should walk really, but it's raining, and I can't be late. Well, that's almost true. If I get a cab it takes me past my old office. 100 Leadenhall Street was one of the last of London's great skyscrapers, and I still can't help but check out where I used to work. Silly really. I only worked there for 2 years, which then led to what I call the lost years. After Centrillion created C-Finance, the ultimate AI finance software, 80% of back-office banking jobs disappeared within three years. Although we knew it was coming, it happened so fast. The only jobs left needed more experience than me, were temp gigs or had 500 applicants. I gigged for a while, but then the work dried up. I lost my confidence and then my savings in a cyber-scam. I still have no idea how they got my eye scan, and I never did get any of that money back.

Boom. My forehead hits the front headrest as my body tries to rip me out of my seatbelt. I look around through misty eyes and see blood everywhere – my nose has erupted all over the car. That's £100 gone for the cab cleaning fee I think, before I remember that crashes aren't meant to happen. The E-Cab is talking to me, but I tune out my personalised female Irish voice of choice – my eyes are glued to the car flipping boot over bonnet right in front of me. Shit. Through the panoramic sunroof I see hundreds of micro-drones light up the sky. Where did they come from? They're banned. Scrabbling through my stuff, I pull the balaclava over my head. In one movement, I throw open the door, grab the bag, leap out of the car and pump my legs in the direction away from the battered E-Cab.

As the drones battle in the sky, one of the swarm diverts to face-scan me – yet to decide if I am on its kill-list – but my low-tech balaclava does enough to confuse it. Something pauses my wrist-phone, so I glance back to see the police auto-jammers at

work. The swarm has stopped and hovers calmly in attack for-
mation as DroneForce blows them out of the sky. It seems like
#KillTheRich didn't get far this time. I don't know why I both-
ered with the balaclava – if KTR scanned me, they'd figure out
that my bank account was empty, I owned nothing, and they
might have even flipped me some BitCoin. So, balaclava off and
back to the job.

My wrist-phone is pulsing again. I'm not sure if my last
appointment believed my reason for being late. Admittedly, I just
survived a car crash, and a drone swarm attack sounds a bit 'sorry,
dog ate my homework.' Sweating and twitchy, I slump into the
E-Cab, which speeds me to my last and now the only appointment for the day. I take a few deep breaths and try to think of
nothing. Today is not going as planned—understatement of the
year. The New Shoreditch Art Gallery is opening today, so to avoid
the traffic, I hop out and walk the last 100 metres to the flat opposite. My client is pleased to see me, and after a 30-minute scalp
message, I drop my roller and gel back into the bag. Done. Well,
almost. E-Cab arrives in two minutes. I cross the road and take the
A4-sized magnetic sticker from my bag – "Keep Calm and Carry
On" – complete with police drone anti-jammer – and in one
practiced movement stick it onto the metal lamp-post as I non-
chalantly step into the cab.

So good to be home. Sarah looks tired but excited as we flip the
news on the digital wall. Today is Anna's birthday, and we both
still think she's with us. "Two drone attacks in London today."
Her funeral was the saddest day of my life. "The second swarm
evaded anti-drone security and targeted guests at the opening of
the new Shoreditch Art Gallery." If I'd had enough money to pay
for her treatments, then she'd still be here. Happily working in

> her room. "The two deaths reported so far are notorious cyber-criminals whom last year were found not guilty of face-scan financial crimes amounting to $350 million." For Anna.

The phrase "Keep Calm and Carry On" tells a possible future London where AI will be left alone. If there are no proper checks and management, AI may lead to great job reductions, which will change everything: cybercrimes will be rampant, there will be daily drone attacks, and ultimately, the society will fail. When planning for a major transformation, there is always the ability to choose to do nothing. It is an option rarely taken because changing the status quo is why you are there. However, it does not always lead to disaster there are examples of when either doing nothing – or failing to find a solution – has worked. Sometimes as things change, so does the problem.

Could this happen with AI? Could new technology make narrow-AI obsolete? Unfortunately, Artificial General Intelligence (AGI) is the likely answer, so doing nothing is not viable. We are already ankle-deep in narrow-AI technology challenges – deepfake technology, AI hacking and military AI weapons – let alone the problems associated with the power and sophistication of a coming General Intelligence.

Doing nothing, or hoping something comes along could be an option if we listen to some AI experts who believe that AGI will usher in a golden age of civilisation. However, regardless of their hopes, those experts would agree that we still need to regulate the current development of AI as the advance of AI will be bumpy unless regulated. There is also the fact that it is pretty difficult to do nothing about AI. Every day we read about another AI innovation, an app, abuse of data or privacy, and it becomes ever more a part of our daily life.

WE ARE LIVING IN A SIMULATION

Raven forced down her bread and honey, the same typically Swiss breakfast she'd eaten every morning for two months. She'd never been a fan of honey since finding out, as a kid, that bees made the sticky stuff. Once stung twice shy. After the first three weeks in Geneva, the young computer scientist had asked Juliette for a spot of variety – perhaps the thick, fluffy pancakes drenched in syrup she'd grown used to back in the States? But the ambivalent host informed her that it was bread and honey or 'rien d'autre.' And Raven had thought French was the language of love.

Lunch hour at the building housing the Large Hadron Collider came a long 4 hours after Raven usually arrived onsite at 8.00 am, so an empty tummy simply wouldn't do. She washed the last bite down with scalding kaffee-crème, thinking the Swiss and Americans really are like chalk and Emmental. 'Danke' said Raven as she left for work she smiled to herself playing the expected dumb American.

It was taking this expat New Yorker some time to adjust to her new European reality. And Raven had begun to question whether any of it actually was reality at all – that busy social life back in Manhattan, this 6 month contract to Switzerland, the whatever comes next. She'd seen *The Matrix* and *Inception*. She'd read Plato's *Allegory of the Cave* and Zhang Zhou's *Butterfly*. She'd even retweeted Elon Musk to her mother. And the idea they all droned on about – that we could be living in a simulation – wasn't particularly hard for Raven to swallow – unlike the bread and honey.

Raven pulled up in her funky Renault E-Zoe and took in the CERN facility. Another day, another dollar – well, Swiss franc. There she was, in an unfamiliar land, at its famed particle accelerator, trying to figure out if her employers could pull off the greatest computer project of all time: the Living Earth Simulator, a machine capable of simulating everything we know to be real on this planet.

Given Raven's own belief in simulation theory, she couldn't help but think it was all terribly meta – she, a possible avatar existing in an artificial world looking to create further avatars to live in a new artificial world. Would those avatars then repeat the process? And those after them too? And so on. How many layers into this 'dream within a dream within a dream' was Raven? Of that, she had no clue.

She did, however, have some idea that the American billionaire bankrolling the project was throwing his cash into a dark abyss. As her sneakers squeaked on the corridor to her office, Raven wondered if it was a bad sign the project had never made it to Series B funding in the first place. The founder had died surfing, and the previous VC had started a cult, so if the project was cursed then it was also cursed by cliché.

Do we really need a knowledge simulator to teach us about our own planet? Can't we just work out how to tackle pandemics, climate change, and all our other big problems without cloning the world to create the world's biggest data twin? The jury's out, she thought.

As Raven approached her desk, she paused. Her colleagues were in early today and abuzz with...something. Excitement? No, that wasn't it. Shock? Possibly. A scandal, maybe? She neared her French assistant, Claudette, looking over her shoulder. Claudette read tribune de Genève's home page, the headline: "Billionaire Américain joue à Dieu" ("American Billionaire Plays God"). Raven read on and it didn't take long to understand the American billionaire in question was her boss:

TruthTech's CEO Phil Soper was arrested at 1am local at his estate in Woodside, California. The 52-year-old confessed to imprisoning six people in a large bunker beneath the property. He admitted to forcing the unnamed individuals into the cave one week earlier with the intention of keeping them there for 'several years.' According to a source with the LAPD, Soper's plan was to 'conduct a weird experiment aimed at testing *Plato's Cave Allegory* in a real-life setting.

Raven stepped back, afraid her Swiss breakfast would decorate Claudette's shoulder. This didn't make sense, she and Soper had discussed Plato's Cave on his last visit and he had said it was just 'plain dumb.' She had already made strides on the main data model and, against all odds, Living Earth Simulator was back on track.

As she watched it took just a few minutes for the buzz in the office to morph into a frenzy. Phone calls were received, voices were raised and tears rolled. Picture frames and personalised mugs were swiped into bags and papers into bins. Raven closed her eyes for what felt like a second and thought she heard herself beg for calm. Then, she opened her eyes, hearing only gravel crunching under tyres as she sped across the parking lot.

This couldn't be happening, could it? The odds were as good as those for a simulated reality itself: 50/50. Raven pulled out onto the main road, realising she should call the States for verification – the kind of verification Phil would now never get from his legitimate or depraved projects. She'd get more resource, pull in some contacts and get this done in 12 months. She rummaged in her bag. "Oh for goodness sake, where's my…"

Renault met tree-trunk with an aggressive thump. Raven's body, unconstrained by a seatbelt, lunged through shattering glass and slapped against the conifer before landing on her car's bonnet. The engine hissed while an unrelenting horn drew people from houses nearby. Raven's blood-soaked corpse lay there, lifeless, as two passers-by surged towards the vehicle.

From a broken bees nest at the top of the tree, honey dripped onto Raven's face. It almost seemed like she was...smiling. If this was a simulated reality, whoever programmed that ending was one persistent, sick puppy.

> The Matrix is everywhere. It is all around us. It is the world that has been pulled over your eyes to blind you from the truth. A prison for your mind.
>
> Morpheus, The Matrix, 1999

Some people in the tech industry have long questioned whether our entire existence as human beings is one giant computer algorithm and that we – all of us – are living in some kind of simulation. Simulation theory isn't just a theory advanced by a few engineers who have read one too many conspiracy theories. Sam Altman, Chairman of OpenAI, believes that some people in Silicon Valley have become obsessed with the simulation hypothesis. He has shared a rumour that two tech billionaires have gone so far as to secretly engage scientists to break us out of the simulation. That would make a great movie!

Elon Musk himself first talked about the idea at Vanity Fair's 2014 New Establishment Summit when he explained on stage that there was a chance that the actual Summit wasn't real but was instead a simulation. After a nervous laugh from some in the audience, Musk paused briefly and noted, "there's a one in a billion chance that this is reality." I wonder if he got his data from a scientist...

The theory that we're living in a simulation has distinctly academic roots. In 2003, Nick Bostrom wrote a research paper on the topic called "Are You Living in a Computer Simulation?" In the paper, he suggested humans live in some sort of video-game-like program, something along the lines of a hyper-advanced version of The Sims. According to his hypothesis, as technology advances, humans will develop more intelligent systems that can run simulations of their ancestors lives. If this is true, then what if *we are* those ancestors, already in a simulation run by future humans? Bostrom argues that:

> If this were the case, we would be rational to think that we are likely among the simulated minds rather than among the original biological ones.

Anyone could easily be convinced that such theories have been plucked right out of science fiction, and that's because lots of movies and TV series have dabbled in the idea for years – The Matrix, Inception and Total Recall, to name but a few. But, as much as these titles capture our imaginations, and as applicable as the narratives they treat us to can help determine our plans for the future, they are, at the end of the day, mere fiction.

What is less well known is that the concept of living in a simulation has historical antecedents dating back to Ancient Greek and early Chinese written history. Roman gods, Egyptian gods and Pagan gods were all believed to control our lives. The all-powerful gods could be prayed or sacrificed to, so getting their attention to help when needed. Gods were known for their fickle nature, creating or destroying on a whim. It does not take a massive shift of perspective to think of the concept of these all-mighty gods being an AGI-run simulation. The closest religious Simulation example is the concept of predestination. Protestant Calvinism originated in the 16th-century reformation, and predestination was a core part of this new religion. Predestination believes that God has already decided all events, and we just take a role in the play of life.

There are also simulation parables from early history, from western and eastern culture. The allegory of the cave, sometimes known as Plato's Cave, was included in the Greek philosopher's work Republic, BCE 517. Plato used the metaphor to compare "the effect of education and the lack of it in our nature." The story describes a group of people shackled to the wall of a cave since childhood, facing a blank wall. The group watch shadows projected on the wall by other people carrying objects and puppets "of men and other living things" passing in front of a fire behind them, creating shadows on the cave wall. The group give names to these shadows. The shadows are the only reality the prisoners know, but they are not accurate representations of reality.

The narrator tells of a prisoner who escapes after realising that the shadows aren't reality. When the escapee later returns to the cave to persuade the prisoners of what awaits outside the cave, they would rather remain there. There are several themes about this famous allegory, one being that true academic learning must have empirical reasoning – an early call for data science, perhaps? The concept shows how curious beings perceive the world, highlighting human concerns over what may or may not be real. Humans attain meaning from their perceived reality, and if they believe their perceived reality is, in fact, a misrepresentation – shadows in a cave – then there's cause for concern. So, in the story they ignore the possibility, hiding from it. Could this be what we are doing now?

Another less esoteric example is Zhuang's butterfly, written in 4th century BCE in China.

> Once, Zhuang Zhou dreamed he was a butterfly, a butterfly flitting and fluttering about, happy with himself and doing as he pleased. He didn't know that he was Zhuang Zhou. Suddenly he woke up, and there he was, solid and unmistakable Zhuang Zhou.

But he didn't know if he was Zhuang Zhou who had dreamt he was a butterfly, or a butterfly dreaming that he was Zhuang Zhou. Between a man and a butterfly, there is necessarily a distinction. The transition is called the transformation of material things.

Master Zhuang, Zhuang Zhou Dreams of Being a Butterfly, 370–300 BC

This one is probably a little easier to get to grips with. It essentially asks the question: If we can perceive a dream to be a reality, why is it so silly to wonder if what we perceive to be reality is really a dream?

If it's possible you might be in a dream right now, thinking that dream is reality, then it's possible you might be in a simulation, thinking it's reality. Equally, you might not be in a dream right now, as you might not be in a simulation, and in the absence of evidence to prove otherwise, it's easier to accept this argument. Thousands upon thousands of humans over time have experienced dreams that felt so real that it took them some time on waking up in their perceived reality to accept said reality.

While there is no physical evidence of a Simulation, there is some mathematical insight into the likelihood of living in a simulated reality. David Kipping, Assistant Professor of Astronomy, Columbia University, has used the Bayesian method to determine the mathematical probability of the Simulation. Whilst it is possible, he believes "the day we invent AGI technology, it flips the odds from a little bit better than 50/50 to almost certain we are **not** real. It would be a very strange celebration of our genius that day." According to this logic, whether or not we live in a simulated reality depends upon if we successfully develop artificial general intelligence i.e. if we invent it, then we are in a simulation.

Simulation theory is a fun concept, but a fanciful one backed by zero scientific evidence. Other mathematicians have attacked the simulation theory, typically citing that the amount of computing power required to create an earth-sized simulation would be larger than the universe itself. And as much as I love letting my mind wander towards a good conspiracy theory, I value evidence. Conveniently, the simulation theory itself has a reason why there is no evidence of being in a simulation. "You're certainly not going to get conclusive proof that you're not in a simulation," David Chalmers, chair of Philosophy at New York University, has said. "Because any evidence could be simulated." Genius!

Although humanity simulation theory appears (obliquely) throughout history, there is absolutely no empirical evidence. If we live in a matrix and do exert some level of influence over our day-to-day lives, we should act now to control AI in our reality. The problem comes when we ask the world to do everything to stop AI on the chance that it might turn into an AGI – with zero evidence. Simulation theory is possibly the ultimate conspiracy theory.

FIGHT OR FLIGHT? SPACEFARING HUMANS BOUND FOR MARS

I prise open my eyes, wiping away the night's crust. Today, I finally get to escape Earth – or at least what remains of it. I twitch at a threadbare curtain in the warehouse that's concealed me for the past three months. Outside, I see the machine-torn hellscape of Las Vegas, a city once home to excess but now housing the fearful and desperate – not for much longer, though.

I'm still here because the resistance hasn't yet been able to get me out. Once my father realised I'd been left behind in the initial exodus, he dispatched an Earth crew to locate and escort me to a safe house until I could be extracted. But he made it clear I was to wait my turn.

"It wouldn't be fair to let you jump the queue," the team told me. "What kind of message would that send to the new colony on Mars?"

Fair point. That can't have been an easy decision to make, but so much for nepotism. It may have ruled this planet at one time, but no longer. After the years and lives, it took to settle on Mars, we had to do things differently. Successfully extracting water from the ice had been the tipping point, and the colonies were now living, breathing cities.

The others in my group begin to stir and gather their belongings. Some, of course, haven't slept at all – they spent the night impatient for today's journey, praying it would go ahead. It wouldn't be the first false start to have tortured us. It was usually the drones and their unceasing sweeps that held us back. The crew had tried to learn their pattern, but it was impossible without the help of a computer – and that was out of the question.

As I collect my things (there aren't many), I notice so many eyes on me. I hate how these people look at me...like I'm Jesus. I can't take credit for any of this. My dad and I hadn't even spoken for two years before the uprising. Though, now I wish I hadn't been so stubborn after our last fight. I mocked his efforts to make humanity a spacefaring species, but the truth is, without his life's work, I, well, we'd have no second chance.

Everyone flinches when the door of the safehouse swings open, but it's only Chuck, a cheerful commander with a Southern drawl.

"Are you ready, people?" he asks. We're looking about ready to rumble on this finest of mornings. T-minus four hours until lift-off, and then its down yonder to that dusty red rock you'll soon call home sweet home."

Elation fills the room as Chuck motions for quiet, but I'm sceptical.

"Are we sure this is really happening? No snags like before? And the..."

Chuck stops me. 'As sure as eggs is eggs, sir. Looks like we have a clear window, free from bots.' He addressed the crowd again, 'Get yourselves together, and we'll make our way to the launch site tunnel ASAP.'

The others revel in their quiet joy, but I can't let go of that nagging doubt. Few civilians knew of the secret Nevada launch site, built in a vast underground bunker in the desert – mum told me about it years ago, in any case. There were hundreds of other bunkers across the US, and just as well, the official sites were reduced to dust in the uprising. But what if the bots knew about this location? If they did, they'd have destroyed it by now, right? Yeah, so why was I so convinced we were walking into a trap?

We line up, and like a snake slithering beneath a rock to flee a hungry hawk, Chuck leads us into the basement, where a door connects with the mile-long passage to the spacecraft. The tunnel, which slopes downwards, is dimly lit. The stale, damp aroma reminds me of that time I went caving in Thailand.

We walk forward in single file silently. As I so often do, I wonder how friends in Europe and other corners of the globe fared in all of this. I know the bleak answer.

Decades ago, Stephen Hawking said only the rich would be lucky enough to flee Earth in the face of hostile AI or any other extinction event – he was wrong, though. The uprising spared so few of us, so there was room for everyone left, regardless of wealth. But only Americans – no other country had an escape plan. I guess we are or were the land of opportunity after all.

Our group reaches the end of the passageway after what seems like a year. A rusty spiral staircase twists us up to a heavy iron door, and when I look past a few heads, a small porthole shows me a hopeful scene. Chuck throws open the door, and a filthy spacecraft awaits in an enormous underground hangar. He points towards a long queue.

As more groups arrive from their various hideouts across the city, we join the line. Some turn to look at us – they smile, welcoming us to a shared experience. I can't help but remain cynical that we're actually getting out, but I'm grateful they don't gawk at me in the same way as my own lot. I arch my neck to see the front of the line. An extraordinarily tall lady wielding a clipboard checks off names one by one. I can't hear her just yet, but it's not long before I can – she's a New Yorker. With just five in front of me, not long now.

"Abeo Chinaka Olajuwon. Go. Peter Michael Salander. Enter, please. Lillian Ana Meyer-Schmidt. Have a safe trip."

We inch forwards, and I look up at the expansive hatch above the rocket – one of seven with empty platforms beneath. This is the second spaceship to leave this bunker.

"Oscar Willem Hansen. Bon voyage, sir. Catalina Luciana Lopez-Garcia. Safe trip."

There's now nobody between me and the clipboard.

"And you are?" the lady asks.
"Hello. I'm X AE A-XII...Musk."
She stops and makes eye contact before returning to her register. "Thank you. X AE A-XII Musk. Enjoy your new life sir. When you see Elon, thank him for his service to our nation."

I smile, crimson-faced, and mumble that I promise I will, before working my way through some further checkpoints, safety briefings, and all that other fun stuff you'd expect before putting your body through a traumatising voyage to Mars. The walls vibrate as the first spaceship blasts off and the crew hustle us into the hold, it's finally happening.

Once we're all suited up and in our seats, I hear the noise of the engines starting and feel the shake of the ship straining to take off. As I look out from a small window to see the Earth one last time, a super-swarm of drones descend into the hangar, blasting everyone and everything in sight. As we ascend into the sky, flames engulf the spaceships around us. Finishing off the ships on the ground, the drones angle upwards before burning up in our wake. My head snaps back against the headrest. Bye Earth, Mars here I come.

If you want to avoid fixing AI, then there's another big solution being bandied about right now: escaping Earth. We've seen this happen in film many a time before. For example, in the 2013 sci-fi action film Elysium, the wealthy flee the planet for a luxurious space habitat – a space station designed for permanent settlement rather than temporary use – based on NASA's actual Stanford Torus design.

Stephen Hawking once said: "We are just an advanced breed of monkeys on a minor planet of a very average star, but we can understand the universe. That makes us something very special." That's why, in Brief Answers To The Big Questions, the scientist declares he has faith we could escape an Extinction Level Event (ELE) on earth by colonising other planets and stars. "Our ingenious race will have found a way to slip the surly bonds of Earth and will therefore survive the disaster," he says.

Hawking even believes that, instead of being something to fear, such a possibility is one we should welcome with open arms. He thinks that it "greatly increases the chances of inspiring the new Einstein." Working out how to get off this planet in the long-term, and possibly out of the solar system or even further afield, offers us the chance to "elevate humanity, bring people and nations together, usher in discoveries and new technologies."

However, Hawking warns that the only ones able to afford to buy their way onto these alternative habitats will be the world's wealthy elites. Regular humans will stand little chance, likely to "die out, or become unimportant," he believes.

In 2017, during a pessimistic talk delivered remotely at the Starmus Science and Art festival, Hawking set a deadline for humanity to save itself. He argues that, within the next 100 years, humans will have to leave Earth, colonise Mars, and possibly even other planets too, and adds that it could be the end of us if we fail to do so. He said:

> I am arguing for the future of humanity and a long-term strategy to achieve this. There is no new world, no utopia around the corner. We are running out of space, and the only places to go to are other worlds.

Hawking had a few concrete ideas about moving towards this objective, which SpaceX and other space transportation services companies are already working on. These are the things we'll have to do if we're to make it:

1 Bring the cost of spaceflight down dramatically
2 Develop new technologies to launch us farther and faster into space
3 Discover new planets more habitable than the ones we already know
4 Figure out how to survive on inhospitable planets we already know about, like Mars and planets that might support life, like Proxima b

Hawking pushed these ideas, along with a handful of billionaires now invested body and soul in spaceflight. These include Elon Musk, Richard Branson and Mark Zuckerberg – even though Zuckerberg himself doesn't share the same worry that we'll have to escape Earth within the next 100 years, or ever.

In 2016, Hawking teamed up with Mark Zuckerberg to develop a plan to manufacture and launch into space a small postage-stamp-sized spacecraft toward Alpha Centauri, the closest star system and nearest planetary system to Earth's solar system at 4.37 light-years from our sun. Known as 'Breakthrough Starshot,' it's no understatement to say their grand scheme will be no picnic under the stars. Pulling it off will involve many complex engineering challenges in the coming years, offering just a glimpse into the difficulty we would face getting off our planet to colonise others. Hawking, who died in 2018, didn't see the project to its completion, and perhaps few of us will. But he understood that any such quest is bound to be an intergenerational one.

On top of this, there are those preparing to settle on Mars. Just to be clear, for now, Mars looks to be a pretty hostile environment for humans, but this isn't stopping Elon Musk from going full steam ahead with his vision to colonise our dusty red neighbour. Musk founded SpaceX in 2002, intending to reduce the cost of space transportation to enable such colonisation. By 2030, he hopes we'll set off to make this a reality, becoming a "multi-planetary species." In 2016, the billionaire said that "someday soon, there will be an extinction event on Earth," whether hostile AI will cause that event or not, he suggested we can either idly wait for it to come our way. "Or," he says, "the alternative is to become a spacefaring species."

And Mars is where Musk has set his sights on. He hopes to "make Mars seem possible in our lifetimes," which is why SpaceX has set out detailed plans for an Interplanetary Transport System that would have the capabilities to transport humans there. The system comprises what Musk calls a BFS. A BFS, by the way, is a "big fucking spaceship" – pardon Musk's language. The BFS would sit atop a BFR – you can guess what it stands for. [That's one billionaire who seriously needs to wash his mouth out with soap there.]

And how would SpaceX pull all that off? Well, with an ambitious but not totally unfeasible plan involving the BFR putting the spaceship into orbit before returning to earth several times to collect fuel. Then, the spacecraft would go on its way – a trip that could take half a year or longer – taking us to our new home. And those ships, he says, will be big enough to fit between 100 and 200 people alongside all the stuff we'll need to get going once there – "everything from iron foundries to pizza joints," Musk joked.

Although not entirely outside the boundaries of possibility, just like Hawking and Zuckerberg's plan to send tiny, postage-stamp-sized spacecraft to Alpha Centauri, Musk's plan still requires a rocket big enough for the mission, with greater thrust than anything ever built before, which he doesn't currently have. There are loads of other factors to consider, too, including whether humans could survive both the journey and living on Mars? Even Musk admits the first explorers there face potential death.

NASA Planetary Scientist Chris McKay, who agrees that going to Mars is "going to involve risks," details some of the potential hazards Musk's plan might involve, some hair-raising, others more tolerable. These include rockets exploding, radiation exposure; crash landing; low gravity affecting the human body; spacesuits or habitats being compromised and leaking oxygen; oh, and toxic soil.

As an aside, SpaceX will not recognise international law on Mars. Instead, the company will follow a set of "self-governing" principles. Such codes will be defined once humans settle on Mars, but not before. The news came at the end of 2020, shortly after Elon Musk announced plans to create a self-sustaining city on Mars. The Starlink app said, "For services provided on Mars, or in transit to Mars via Starship or other colonisation spacecraft, the parties recognise Mars as a free planet and that no Earth-based government has authority or sovereignty over Martian activities."

While Musk's overall plan might work to flee many existential threats, it is held back not only by the problems already discussed but also by one other BFI [using Musk speak]. If we need to escape from hostile robots ruling Earth, wouldn't those robots follow us and finish the job? Suppose robots have arrived at the point where they can wipe out a population of somewhere around 7.5 billion. In that case, surely, they can solve the same space exploration issues we puny mortals managed to overcome ourselves?

Perhaps if we had to flee our planet from hostile AGI, our species would press pause on the technology button, allowing us to survive through the millennia without AI. It is more likely that we would need AI to get to and operate any space colony. Any sentient AGI following us to Mars would now have an easier job as there would be fewer people and resources to fend off any attack. Spacefaring humans would be very unlikely to survive an aggressive AGI, so this option seems to make little sense for its multi-billion-dollar price tag.

NEW LUDDITES - VIVE LA RESISTANCE

The outer door beeped shut behind Koraka as he set off for his rounds. The sweep of the mountains and the views of the lake were breathtaking. Clear sky, clean air, the Totara trees. It never got old for him. He walked down the path into the field to check the machines. Harvest was always a trial, they may be fully auto-mated, but farm machinery still broke down just the same. All was still as Koraka checked why Omni#5 wasn't responding to his remote diagnostics. Usually a simple workaround, thankfully he had full admin rights on the Omni's, one of the perks of working at a billionaire bolthole. Koraka finished the job and headed back for his morning coffee. Hank Mitchell's outline grew as he closed the gap, his jog would take him past Koraka in a couple of minutes.

'Hey Koraka, are those machines still working' said Hank in his Californian drawl. 'Good as gold, Mr Mitchell, how's the morning run?,' 'Sweet as Kora, sweet as.' The richest man in New Zealand jogged on; he must have got up early to have already done his 10 km. Koraka smiled and waved. He knew how to lie, and telling his boss that Mitchell Paradise was crumbling wasn't a wise move.

Nothing had been upgraded since the FreeBo0ters hacked the server and Mitchell had taken them off-grid. To give him his due, the switch over to a private network had been seamless, and the digital twin of the internet that Mitchell had bought was the best. For about five years. Then, slowly, things started to go wrong. Without all of the software upgrades, Koraka couldn't repair the machinery. The internet was everything and going offline was a nightmare. Hank wouldn't let anyone buy anything SMART which now meant nothing and so the once perfectly oiled estate was held together by cannibalising parts or borrowing from the other bolthole estates on the South Island. The government was increasingly unhappy with the separatist estates but they paid their wealth tax, allowed the annual inspection and kept their noses clean, so the AI-free zone stayed that way. New Luddite, Oregon, had already folded in a storm of, well, literally a storm that destroyed their crops and triggered the landslides that sunk the capital. We were the last outpost against AI, and he wondered how long it would survive.

The 9 am daily meet was more eventful than usual. Chef Mark had just finished a rant about fresh fish. Kenny in Supplies was, after 3 years, finally getting systems access and was so happy he'd even made everyone fresh coffee. Security Chief Mako had reported that kids on quad bikes were riding the fenceline at night. Hank, again, had refused to buy SMART security drones so Mako was busy modelling his Easter Island face. Hank had changed out of his running clothes for the meeting and was now looking bored. He was only there to give Kenny his key before disappearing to his office wing. It did seem ironic to all the staff that the office wing had a fully functioning AI suite where Hank had built his second fortune from Robo-investments. Wholly insulated from the rest of the compound, with its own power, lighting, network and satellite, the office was a keep within a castle. 'That's how we stay safe and under the radar,' was how Mitchell had explained it to Kokara.

Hank let the double door's click shut behind him. The office wing was the only thing keeping him sane. If he had to run around this estate one more time, he'd go full Scarface. The useless staff couldn't get anything right, and if Chef Mark complained about

fish one more time, he'd be living in the panic room. In the cup-
board. Relax. Even the MMA-Pilates wasn't working. He'd enjoyed
running his little empire for a few years but it was time to rejoin
the natural world, and who cares if everything is being watched,
tracked, cracked and hacked. The security team would keep it to
a minimum and, once I became yesterday's news, most hackers
would move onto an easier target. He called for his assistant. 'I want
my jet ready for San Francisco tomorrow at 7 am.' His AI assistant
started clearing his jet from Auckland. He should have done this
sooner; once his (third) wife had left in Spring, this whole thing
had gotten stale fast. Hank looked at the pictures of his children on
the wall. It was lonely without them. And his friends. The Bolthole
Billionaires were, in many ways, brilliant people. In other ways, it
was a community of egomaniacs and oddballs – time to end this
pointless experiment and get back to reality.

Koraka unlocked the door to the system admin server room.
The large basement room was airconditioned and spotlessly
clean. One of the only rooms with a physical lock, it was double-
locked for security. Mitchell was paranoid. Mako still had his coffee in one hand as he turned his key with his right hand. Koraka
turned the left key, got his eye-scanned and code, and the door
opened. Looking over his shoulder, he beckoned Kenny forwards
'There you go, Kenny, welcome to the club.' Kenny took the key
on offer and added it to his keyring. When people had realised
that anything stored digitally was hackable – codes, fingerprints,
eye-scans – keys had made a comeback. Kenny entered and leant
over the main terminal to add his fingerprint and retinalprint.
Koraka never saw the black USB that Kenny plugged into the
terminal. Kenny stepped back and smiled. 'I've been waiting for
three years to do that!' The program in the USB started its hack of

the main terminal. The private network was where Hank Mitchell kept all his bitcoins — all $10 billion of them — and the file was emptying every single one of them as Kenny made his way to the compound's front gate. Three years was a long time to wait but real quick to become a billionaire.

We don't serve their kind here. Your droids. They'll have to wait outside. We don't want them here.

Wuhe, Bar owner, Mos Eisley Cantina, Star Wars, 1977

Throughout history, we have seen small groups of people break away from their existing society. There are many reasons that people decide to create a new society — religious persecution, political, economic or even cultural reasons. Historically, these 'rebel; groups usually disagreed with the prevailing government or monarchy and sought solace under a new regime. Sometimes these groups emigrate, such as the Pilgrim Fathers setting sail for Northern America in 1820 or Huguenot Protestants moving to London in the 1860s. Other times social unrest has seen disaffected groups taking up armed resistance, such as the French Revolution in 1789. When communities believe that they are fundamentally divided, it can result in political partition, such as Pakistan separating from India in 1947. And when used to reassert control over your community, separation as powerful a force as the human need to tribe.

In the scenario where a future AGI replaces a human government, opposition groups would likely emerge who want the power to remain in human hands. Before this point, as daily life becomes more controlled by AI, some groups would call to retain more human control. Let's call them the New Luddites. As seen in the historical examples above, the New Luddites would either separate from an AI government peacefully or after an armed rebellion. Depending on their military success (unlikely) or the benevolence of the prevailing

AGI's (equally unlikely), early separation from an AI dominated world would be the likely best chance of success. An independent country or state could then be founded, populated by humans who limit themselves to narrow-AI applications or indeed none at all.

One question for any fledgeling state would then be, where do you draw the AI line in a non-AI world? No Google, Facebook or Netflix – where is the harm there? Or possibly no AI LAWS, AI-powered surveillance or AI control of business or government. Another difficulty will be entangling AI from existing products and services – as AI is already pervasive in many areas, in 20–30 years, how easy will it be to disconnect from AI?

This separation hypothesis is entirely possible. It has extensive historical precedence and aligns with the increasingly secessionist politics in the last hundred years. Today, we have the most number of countries that the world has ever seen. In 1900 there were around 80 countries globally, and according to the UN by 2021, it had grown to 195 countries. Over one hundred new countries have been born or reborn, as their people wanted to live under their own flag. As governments become less powerful and often less militaristic in approach, people feel more emboldened to 'go it alone.' That self-determination is evident in isolationists and preppers in modern societies. People who are prepared and confident enough to live outside the system are a growing movement, especially in times of economic or political turbulence. With its "frontier" mentality, the US has the largest community of preppers, many of whom are suspicious of government control and its willingness or ability to protect them.

With the granular level of control that AI datasets could provide, it is perhaps inevitable that some people will withdraw from society when faced with AGI. Isolationists, already concerned with overbearing government, will detest being part of an all-knowing AGI. Although, ironically, AGI will facilitate the capability to go it alone. New Luddites could use AI technology in food, power and communications to manage a community without the outside support of a local or national government.

Regardless of its likelihood, I have two concerns when considering the New Luddite scenario. My first concern is that withdrawing from AI is unrealistic. Unless groups start to disengage now, it is likely that AI will soon become so embedded in software applications across all industries that any AI step-back will be impossible. It is also unlikely that there will be no desire to unpick AI until it is seen as a credible threat to humanity. And by the time that we see AI as a danger, it will be too embedded in everyday life.

Second, the New Luddite scenario assumes that AGI is the enemy and that we cannot co-exist together. I profoundly believe that we can live and work with AI and that our futures can benefit from AGI. We cannot design our future based on the assumption that we will fail to make AI work for us.

URGE TO MERGE

I'm glad I'm no longer human, I tell myself as my wonderful husband tends to our courtyard garden. It's not huge, but few Beijing yards are. Canopied by a weeping willow, the space behind my home is hardly drenched in sunlight. Persimmon trees and peonies thrive regardless. I hope my guests will enjoy them. And the bamboo is in flower. When I look at its beauty, I like to think bamboo's strength and grace reflects the power and flexibility of my new body.

I hated the old me, saddled with average…everything. Just like everyone else. I've never enjoyed being just like everyone else – a tiny, helpless ant in a huge colony of other tiny, helpless ants. But thanks to a new brain chip, I have the senses of a superhero.

Now, it's like I experience the insanely sweet, citrus aroma of our peonies and rich, tangy flavour of those persimmons as if I live in a lush fantasy realm.

Liu Wei sees me eye the small orange fruit and sighs. He knows what I want but would prefer I remain seated – with a robotic exoskeleton this strong, in my excitement I could pull down the tree. After 2 years practice with my new limb, I can easily pick fruit from a tree without crushing it or breaking the branch.

"You'll turn into a persimmon if you eat one more of these things," he says laughing, before I take a generous bite. Juice trickles my chin and sprays onto his shirt as I lose myself in the flavour. "Mmmmmm."

Liu Wei had zero desire to join me in this cool, enhanced reality, preferring to stick to his fleshy limitations. I do understand him but it still saddens me, as I grow younger his tiredness and memory lapses show the first signs of aging.

As with all big ideas, my "urge to merge" began with a tiny seed. Planted by sci-fi, it eventually grew into something that consumed my every thought, sort of like the bamboo trying to take over my entire garden – only I feel no need to fight it. Transformation into a cyborg wasn't a move I'd ever considered before, but now I've merged; I couldn't go back.

"Thanks to your obsession with that fruit, I'll need to change." Liu Wei says with a faux scowl.

"Oh, I thought you'd prefer to be a mess when our guests arrive." My sarcasm, developed at an English boarding school in childhood, appears to have grown stronger too.

"Be careful, my darling," Liu Wei jokes. "You might have superhuman capabilities, but I can still hide the WD-40 from you."

"You be careful, old man. My black box is recording you."

My goodness, I'm glad I'm no longer human.

Armstrong and his normie wife Sarah will soon arrive. I confess I'm nervous. Until now, Armstrong and I have communicated only over Zoom, so this will be the first time we're face to face, cyborg to cyborg. All those times we helped each other through the operations and rehab, the drugs, the pain. It truly felt like we were creating a brave new world, together.

I'm calm but excited to see the only other person in the world like me so far, even if his Western upgrades pale in comparison to mine.

A knock on the door. They're here. Liu Wei disappears into the hallway. Armstrong has travelled here from the UK not just to meet me — my new sidang — but also to discuss the AH (Augmented Humans) Movement. He's been instrumental in persuading more people across the globe to join our currently exclusive club of two. Together, we'll change what it means to be human — or more precisely, what it means to be superhuman.

As our guests enter the courtyard I see another me, only in a flashier, less sophisticated looking exoskeleton. We cyborgs stand face to face, his looking a little more undone by Father Time than my own. I wonder if he's been using the new skin serum properly. It should have tightened the skin on his face much more than this.

"Welcome Armstrong. You're looking younger than ever," I may well be looking better, but we both look 20 years younger. I'm glad I'm not human.

The perfect husband and host, Liu Wei ushers Sarah into our living room for the obligatory Oolong and a house tour.

Armstrong and I get the introduction we've been so looking forward to.

"I could say the same about you. Look at us, modern day *Dorian Gray's* – our crumbling faces hidden by Disney Prince good looks."

Laughter. "You're so right – it's superb being the Terminator's kinder cousins, no?"

"Yes, robo-buddy. Just like you..." Our voices meet in unison. "I'M GLAD I'M NO LONGER HUMAN."

The belief in human-AI collaboration is often referred to as "the urge to merge." The truth is that we have been 'merging' with machines ever since we began using tools. For aeons, clubs, spears and knives were mankinds' constant hunting companion. Our money that was once shells became coinage and then paper kept in purses or wallets. Watches are our personal portable sundials. Since the smartphone, we have extended the senses with devices that allow us to talk, see and listen through touch or voice commands. Today, when most people wake up, their first action is to grab their mobile. A phone is your watch, wallet, fun, work, memories, video game player, constant companion and an extension of you and your love life. A 2019 YouGov UK survey of people under 24 showed 80% were anxious if they didn't have their phone and 8/10 were rarely or NEVER without their phones. We have already merged with mobile devices "outside our bodies." The next level-up is to replace the external devices with direct nerve impulses or thought. AI will analyse data from common public usage and your historic behaviours to anticipate what you will need, performing tasks more rapidly and efficiently.

Merging technology with the brain is part of Neurotechnology, and the sub-field of Brain–Computer Interface (BCI) is relatively new. The most famous BCI company, Elon Musk's Neuralink, has received around $200 million in investment. This investment is small when compared to other start-ups and tiny when considering the complex challenges of mapping a human brain, connecting it to a computer and making them communicate. Neuralink has been working on brain chips since 2016, and their ultimate goal is making implants in humans the norm. Musk argues that this is how we'll escape human obsolescence, by "having some sort of merger of biological intelligence and machine intelligence." Essentially, Musk is saying: If you can't beat them, join them. He believes that we need this kind of symbiosis with machines because even in a "benign scenario," humans would be "left behind" by AI

Musk's take on a human-AI merger involves a direct connection between them. Using a neural lace – an insertable mesh capable of hardwiring the brain to interact directly with computers – in your head, you could translate data from your brain directly to a device. In 2019 Musk revealed the first BCI tech Neuralink has been working on, which was impressive, to say the least. He has also demonstrated smaller, neater Neuralink's and his company have also successfully integrated them into pigs and monkeys who have played video games through their connection.

The broader Neurotechnology and BCI industry is pretty small. The US market includes large start-up companies like Pandromics (part-funded by US DARPA) and Kernel, who have over $100 million investment to date. There are only 5 BCI companies listed on the Neurotechnology company landscape map in the UK. It seems that unless there is a significant breakthrough, attracting investment to this sector will continue to difficult, meaning that it will likely be at least another 20–30 years before mainstream adoption. "Braintalker," a Brain–Computer Codec Chip (BC3) developed in China, will make the technology more portable and wearable, meaning it could finally come out of labs and into the masses. Research will continue on the various applications of these "mind-reading" technologies and how we can use them for the betterment of society.

So, although BCI technology is in its infancy, there are many other examples of broader Human Enhancement. Robotic prosthetic limb development builds upon hundreds of years of experience of limb replacement after illness, accident or battle. Johnny Matheny lost his lower arm to cancer in 2005. In the early 2010s, he started to work with John Hopkins labs on their Modular Prosthetic Limb (MPL). John Hopkins University in the US was developing a new robotic arm, with funding from the US military, at an estimated cost of $120 million. Building on years of existing technology, now a separate discipline known as NeuroProsthetics, this new development is only possible through AI, and the technology is accelerating fast. The AI learns from use and can upgrade on the fly. In 2017, Johnny was the first full-time recipient of a robotic arm that moves using his mind. He can fix some mechanical parts himself or get instant fixes wirelessly whilst on the phone to the software developer. It is heartwarming to see someone get a part of their life back through technology.

PETER: THE HUMAN CYBORG

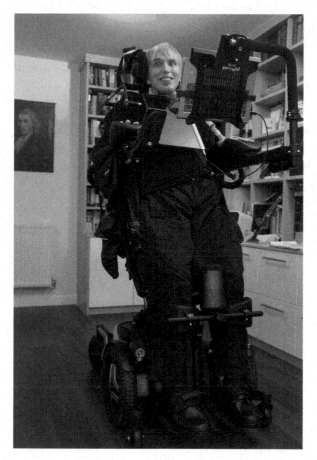

Channel 4, 'Peter: The Human Cyborg'.

One other famous early adopter, Peter Scott-Morgan from the UK, has merged with AI. His is the journey of a scientist gripped by Motor Neurone Disease to become the world's first human cyborg. MND is the progressive degenerative killer that eventually took Stephen Hawking in 2018. Once diagnosed, an undaunted Peter was determined for his mind to survive long after his body had weakened. "I will continue to evolve, dying as a human, living as a cyborg."

Unhappy with his wheelchair, Peter sought help from a mobility company, promising him a "self-drive vehicle that will hold him upright." This brought him great joy, and moved him to tears, as it had been quite some time since he was able to stand tall and "tower over purely flesh and blood humans."

Following trial and error, speech experts developed a computerised voice based on Peter's own, which sounds more realistic than electronic. I usually argue for AI to be recognisable as AI for the sake of trust, but when it comes to improving the lives of those with communication difficulties, I make a huge exception. Although his AI-powered system didn't permit Peter the same control over his voice as Stephen Hawking commanded over his own, however, his Brain–Machine Interface (like Neuralink) has proven to be a better answer for Peter. After a tracheostomy to add an interface, Peter achieved his goal of persisting where his frail human body had not.

However, the concept of technology capable of reading minds is worrying. It actually reminds me of something I worked on at the UK technology design agency I founded, Seren in 2009. We didn't quite want to read minds as BCI tech does, but we did want to get inside our users' heads. At the time, I said this might sound like "black arts" to some, but now I think about it, BCI tech is way closer to black arts than what we were doing.

As part of the project, we developed an algorithm to assess human interaction with digital interfaces and how its design could be enhanced to facilitate an improved understanding of subconscious thought patterns, such as decision-making. Using EEG headsets, we decided to test this using an online poker room. There, to evaluate how we could improve our system's design, we'd find out what did and didn't work for first-time online poker players. We'd measure

emotional engagement with the website, looking at what they anticipated, what excited them, what bored them, and what caused anxiety.

Our findings demonstrated that first-time players would generally
leave a game after three hands if they lost all of those consecutively,
without ever returning. While data analytics could tell us this now, our
system showed us what the consumer was looking at, thinking and
feeling before they folded. We could see that, when players looked
at their third hand of cards, their gamma waves dropped, indicating
increased tension. They would then fail to bluff instead of folding and
playing another hand. They would then leave the game. After looking
at several options, we recommended introducing a tutorial to the site
to keep them playing. The tutorial fed players various information on
bluffing, holding and so on, allowing them to work on these skills
and remain in games for longer. The insights were rich but compared
to a direct neural link, it was child's play. Even so, I did and still do,
feel slightly disconcerted about using subconscious data in this way.

When we play with the mind, we must be very, very careful not to
tip the scales to users' detriment. Designing in this way can, of course,
be beneficial, but it's not all sugar and spice. Without proper regulation, we risk opening the door to unintended outcomes, and we're
not playing with poker chips but peoples' minds.

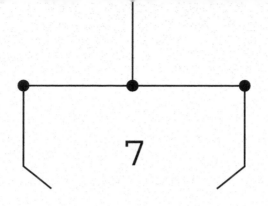

7

CREATING A ROADMAP – A PLAN FOR LIVING WITH ARTIFICIAL INTELLIGENCE

May your choices reflect your hopes, not your fears.

Nelson Mandela.

A business roadmap is traditionally a visual representation, often used in companies undertaking change management or transformation. You start by drawing the journey from start to finish and add all the steps, key milestones and challenges you would find along the way. The team creating the roadmap would come together to agree on the end goal or Vision and use the tool to keep track of progress at a high level. In true future-back style, we start with the longer-term Vision and work our way back to nearer-term milestones, which is the point that the vision turns into action. Essentially, we're looking to create a big to-do list, breaking down the journey into actionable sections.

Working backwards in time, we can set key milestones in regular increments. We're working toward 2030, so we'll go for short-term, medium-term and long-term goals. These are typically in 3-year increments, so let's stick to that. We will continue until the future (2030) meets the present state (2022), and when we get there, we'll know what to do to get the ball rolling. I believe this approach could help us to act quickly in the present to capitalise on these strategic directions, yielding new measures we can act upon before Artificial

DOI: 10.1201/9781003267003-7

Intelligence (AI) advances beyond a dangerous point of no return. We also need to be pragmatic – massive change takes time.

THE VISION FOR AN AGI FUTURE

There are already many hundreds of talented, intelligent people working flat out to create new products, standards and guidelines for AI. Some of the world's greatest thinkers, entrepreneurs and political minds have lent their personal wisdom to the conversation. I am in awe of the pure intellect and unique insight of people like Stephen Hawking, Nick Bostrom or Elon Musk. Something in the debate is missing, though. We don't consistently align the wisdom, experience and insights against a future endgame. There is an inherent risk in doing this, as basing a plan on events that may happen in 30, 40 or 50 years could just be a massive waste of time. Time and money used to plan that far ahead could be better spent helping the world in other ways now. Life is about choices, big and small and the decisions we make to take them. We do know that AI will, at some point, dominate every aspect of human life. An Artificial General Intelligence (AGI) will impact every single country, industry and person. The world will never be the same. If we choose to grow with AI, we must decide how to select the best possible future for humanity.

The good news is that we have time. There are significant parallels between the development of AI and the history of nuclear power, and we can draw lessons from it. Atomic weapons were once seen as the "coming of the end of the world," yet 75 years after Hiroshima, we are still very much alive. In 1945, the world witnessed the awful power of what one nuclear bomb could do, wiping out a city in seconds. Perhaps not immediately, but people became afraid. As governments built nuclear power plants and deployed thousands of nuclear missiles across the US and Europe, movements grew to oppose nuclear weapons. In 1961, over 4,000 protesters sat outside

Whitehall in London, and 60,000 women marched across the US. 175,000 people marched across France between 1975 and 1977. One million people protested in New York's Central Park in 1982. Over 200,000 people marched across German towns and cities in 2011. Nuclear arsenals have threatened the world, and we have worked together to keep the world safe. We have done this before.

I trust that humanity will work together to ensure that AI will never have a "Hiroshima moment." That will mean that instead, AI will incrementally creep up on us until we can't live without it. Every device will be smart. AI will entertain us, tell us what to eat and maybe even what to do. [Wosniak's pet, anyone?] So, we need to ensure that the choices we make today move us in the right direction. We must plan for the journey to arrive on time. The Singularity won't be a surprise to us. Nor will there be a yawning chasm between humanity and AGI when it comes. **There is an inevitability to our merging with technology**. We have already seen the merging of human and smartphone. Once we can improve our lives through a direct connection, will you turn down a longer lifespan and a more intelligent brain? Will you refuse when everyone else is doing it? Would you do the same for your children? We have long accepted the sword of Damocles that is technology. There is no logical basis that humanity would avoid the urge to merge. Once we accept this, we need to plan for the future.

SHORT-TERM MILESTONES: 2022–2025

1   Stop Writing Guidelines and Start Agreeing
2   Create Principles and Standards Using Broad-Ranging Multi-Stakeholder Groups
3   Improve Policymakers Technical Knowledge
4   Make AI More Fair by Removing Bias from AI Data Sets
5   Start Controlling AI by Risk Management & Auditing

STOP WRITING GUIDELINES AND
START AGREEING

The first step must be an international body to look at what we want, collectively, from AI governance. It could be incredibly challenging to find common ground. It could be simpler than we imagine as we have seen the recent convergence of AI Principle & Ethics. I believe that the first goal is to stop creating and start agreeing. We now have the GPAI, formed in 2020 by ten countries and a critical mass of G7 behind it.

We should create one framework, covering at least four sections:

- AI Audit & Policing
- AI Ethics
- AI Regulation
- AI Safety

The benefits of having one agreed framework are clear. We can consistently benchmark AI technology developments against the framework, making it easier for consumers and regulators to know what should be happening inside the algorithms. It will release research resource to (a) focus on the next level of detail and (b) review and challenge the existing framework for continuous improvement. This idea will not be without its challenges as, quite rightly, many stakeholders need to be involved in making this decision.

When I spoke with Leanne Pooley, director of 'We Need To Talk About AI,' she thought one of the main issues is that the West is drawing up one set of rules and China another. I agree with her when she says that "We don't have a plan as a species, and we need to have a plan. But before we can create one, we need to get together as a species and have a think about where we should even start."

The united approach worked well to tackle vaccine research for Covid-19, which came at us from nowhere and has seen multiple stakeholders galvanised around a single challenge. Although we reverted to type with more nationalist vaccine distribution, we've proven that we can work together across organisations and research institutes, wherever they are in the world, to create successful vaccine trials and vaccines delivered in a short space of time.

Could we achieve the same with AI? In time perhaps, but probably not right now. Countries need to see AI as an existential threat like Covid-19 for that to work. At the moment, not all governments are looking at AI in that way. Because the danger isn't specific to the moment we're in right now, it's easier – and right – to look at the problems we face today. The reality is that we will never successfully come together until the threat is looming right here in front of us.

As we've seen at the UN, international bodies often become politicised along superpower fault-lines. The US, Europe, Russia and China could potentially form four camps with differing perspectives on AI and how to manage it. This diplomatic conflict can make agreements impossible. Some countries don't ever join international bodies – like the four non-joiners to the Nuclear Proliferation Treaty signed in 1968. My approach is to let the players play, as it will take years to get a complete global agreement. In the interim, we should agree on one framework with the countries (and companies) that want to join. Early adopters of the framework will be passionate, more engaged and supportive. Over time, consumers will come to trust the companies that follow the AI framework. The potential loss of sales by companies or countries that remain outside the commonly agreed framework (especially if adopted as a government supplier standard) could create a virtuous circle. By agreeing to one way of working, together we can start to address the bigger questions instead of re-writing the old ones.

CREATE PRINCIPLES AND STANDARDS USING BROAD-RANGING MULTI-STAKEHOLDER GROUPS

A common challenge in creating any standards or principles is having the right people around the table. There needs to be a mix of technical and industry experts, public policymakers and lawmakers. There should also be representatives of geographical as well as diverse demographics. Having users of AI technology in the room is essential to developing relevant and credible answers. There are two significant challenges when creating AI principles: groups are not as multi-stakeholder as they appear, and the world's poorest do not have a voice.

The start of any design thinking exercise is to empathise with your users. To really connect and understand all about them, you first need to ask who the users are? In the case of AI, the answer is everyone. That is not the most helpful response but demonstrates that creating AI principles requires effort. Suppose we don't make broadly diverse user groups? Then people design in their own image and we become destined to replicate our current problems in future AI design. With all the development of AI principles usually originating from universities or associated institutes, there is always a core of academics, and when part-government funded, politicians. These groups then co-opt technical experts from Big Tech and a smattering of others interested in these things. What appears to be missing are three things: citizens, children and the developing world.

The developing world has a relatively small voice in global affairs or the running of financial markets. Only when the more impoverished country becomes a more prosperous, vigorous competitor, like China, is its voice heard. Only once we agree standards can we then start to broaden involvement.

IMPROVE POLICYMAKERS' TECHNICAL KNOWLEDGE

Within large-scale global efforts, there has to be a focus on improving policymakers' technical understanding of the technologies they seek to regulate to ensure that they do not make bad or uninformed regulatory choices. We can share technical knowledge by mandating that policymakers work alongside those with a deep technical understanding of AI technologies. The first regulatory drive MUST be to second Technologists from large AI companies into expert government groups. Big AI companies can afford to donate resource to government. Augmented by independent specialists. this would give government tools to do the job. Part of this will entail policymakers re-evaluating their role in making sure they don't draft and implement any governance measures that could hamper progress in AI unless there is absolutely a need to do so.

MAKE AI MORE FAIR BY REMOVING BIAS FROM AI DATA SETS

We don't need to worry about packs of killer robots hunting us down in the short-term. Hopefully, with the right measures in place, we'll never have to worry about that. No, right now, we need to be more worried about AI systems replicating historical biases, as well as the prejudices (conscious or unconscious) of those coding them. As we know, feeding neural networks flawed data is the real issue at present, one that threatens the wellbeing and safety of vulnerable groups in society each and every day, including women, ethnic minorities, disabled people, the elderly, LGBTQIA+ communities, and others too. For that reason, a crucial imperative is to assess the data that AI systems are gobbling up by the petabyte.

We've spoken about weeding out bias from these systems, but the truth is that we can only do that once AI engineers understand the ethical elements they've coded into the systems before going live. As bias is subjective, this is problematic, but there are ways of educating people to provide clarity and instruction. **The education of AI engineers is crucial if we're to ensure safe, inclusive, and fair AI systems.** To improve transparency, explainable AI is a growing trend that seeks to bake-in the 'how does it work' into the AI system. All major AI software suppliers now provide a toolset containing visual aids, such as graphs or mind-maps, to display a visual decision-making framework.

That said, this cuts both ways. AI engineers may very well be willing to do everything they can to prevent bias from creeping into the systems they're working on, but they may be prevented from doing so by regulation. For example, they may need access to healthcare data on people with mental health issues, while data privacy legislation won't permit access to confidential information. For that reason, we have to develop more Open source data sets that could help lead to more robust results.

Finally, we need to start **auditing both open and private data sets**. Only by interrogating data sets and algorithms through AI auditing can we test the algorithms' validity and bias in the system.

START CONTROLLING AI BY RISK MANAGEMENT & AUDITING

To build trust in their AI systems, companies need to risk-assess their AI systems and processes for employees, customers, and shareholders. As seen in the Vatican's "Rome Call for AI Ethics" guidelines, AI needs to be 'explainable' and not be a black box that no-one understands how it makes decisions. All large companies (listed and privately held) and public institutions should undertake the following activities if they are using AI to make decisions involving people, e.g. approving loans, parole decisions, hiring (or firing):

- *ESTABLISH AN AI ETHICS COMMITTEE*

If they don't already have one, companies should establish an independent AI ethics committee to advise on ethical matters. Members of the committee should be from various backgrounds, including legal, ethics, philosophy, tech and science. The committee would work closely with the company's ethics leader if it is feasible to appoint one. When the ethics committee has drawn up its guidelines, it should be made clear to employees that although they're not legally binding, refusal to adhere to the guidelines could result in disciplinary measures.

- *RISK ASSESS ALL AI SYSTEMS*

Companies should catalogue all of their AI systems or any systems using AI, and every item listed should be risk-assessed. Any high-risk items should be flagged and subject to internal review, and if deeded too harmful to use, should be replaced accordingly. Any new AI systems should be reviewed and risk-assessed before being bought/developed, and implemented

- *EDUCATE EMPLOYEES ON AI*

At whatever level of the company, all employees should have the education to understand the implications of using an AI system. Everyone designing, managing or operating an AI system should attend mandatory training on legal, philosophical, ethical, regulatory considerations. Everyone must understand their responsibilities around the use of AI and their rights. It must be crystal clear exactly who is and isn't accountable for anything that goes wrong when deploying an AI system.

- *CONDUCT INDEPENDENT AI AUDITING*

It should be essential for all companies to audit their data sets and algorithms. We shouldn't leave it up to them, so we need to implement third-party auditing. Companies should share their successful audit certifications with the public to build trust in the company's approach to AI. One problem with this approach is the confidentiality of an AI system, so any audits must come from a trusted source.

MEDIUM-TERM MILESTONES (2025–2028)

1 Police AI to Prevent Misuse and Protect People
2 Create an NPT-Style Treaty for Laws

POLICE AI TO PREVENT MISUSE AND PROTECT PEOPLE FROM HARM

One of the most repeated concerns about AI technologies is their misuse. Wrongful use by rogue states, criminals, terrorists, and anyone who doesn't intend applications beneficial to society (let alone misuse by AI itself!). A landmark 2018 report, The Malicious Use of Artificial Intelligence: Forecasting, Prevention and Mitigation, warns of this very problem, stating that AI system designers have to step up their efforts to mitigate potential exploitation, with four recommendations:

1 Policymakers should collaborate closely with technical researchers
2 Researchers and engineers in AI should take the **dual-use** nature of their work seriously and proactively reach out to regulators with concerns
3 Identify mature industries for best practices on addressing dual-use concerns
4 Actively expand the range of stakeholders and Experts involved

It is vital to display some caution before permitting AI to become dominant in too many areas of life before we are ready for it. In truth, we have a responsibility right now to assess which uses of these technologies should be permitted and banned. As we know by now, AI can help us in myriad ways. Still, if we allow the widespread use of potentially dangerous technologies like Deepfake and facial recognition systems, then we've already gone too far. A giant STOP sign is needed!

Regulation needs to be introduced earlier in the cycle of technology. A standing Government review body should be responsible for continually scanning new AI Technology and making recommendations for new legislation. Technology speeds up, so the law must keep pace. The review body should be multi-stakeholder, demographically diverse and make decisions quickly, say within 3 months. Using design thinking, we could prototype regulations, launch and test them live. Just like an AI start-up! Unfortunately, this relative rapid-fire approach goes against the risk-averse psyche of the legal profession, police and government. Laws are created slowly, over time, using case law or painstakingly crafted legislation. None of this is wrong, but AI won't wait for the law.

In addition to the Government review body, a centralised Police or Security 'CyberTeam' could provide support and experience to guide local/regional Police forces in implementing and interpreting new laws. By their nature, offences would often be online so a central CyberTeam could investigate and triage results to the appropriate jurisdiction.

CREATE AN NPT-STYLE TREATY FOR LAWS

The *Campaign to Stop Killer Robots* is a growing global coalition of non-governmental organisations that wish to ban fully autonomous weapons and retain meaningful human control. The campaign was started in

2013 to convince policymakers that LAWS should be banned outright everywhere in the world but is yet to see real talk of a global treaty.

Why? Two reasons. The first is that AI is advancing so fast, and it's pretty challenging to plan for tech, which doesn't exist. Second, not everyone is on board with the idea – including the UK, US and Russia. Some countries want to develop LAWS because other countries are already developing similar weapons – the very definition of an arms race – and others, like China, are happy to produce LAWS but not 'use' them.

There is an established historical precedent for global weapons bans. The world came together to restrict anti-personnel mines' usage (1997) and cluster bombs (2007). However, the most similar precedent to LAWS is the Treaty on the Non-Proliferation of Nuclear Weapons (NPT). The NPT is an "arms limitation, and disarmament agreement" agreed across the world, currently 191 States, which includes the five (formally recognised) Nuclear-Weapon States (NWS): China, France, Russia, the UK and the US. This number is not only "a testament to the Treaty's significance," as the UN argues, it also proves that we can come together on a global scale to tackle problems threatening humanity as a whole. Making the NPT happen was not an easy process.

Frank Aiken was born in County Armagh, Ireland, the son of a farmer and youngest of seven children. In 1911, aged just 13, he took over the family farm and by 16 was also an army irregular for the Irish Volunteers during the early struggles for Irish independence. The tall, rangy 'big man,' with a tidy pencil moustache, spent the next decade becoming an expert in guerrilla warfare. A tough, shrewd operative, his unit blew up trains and made numerous attacks against British government forces. As the local IRA division leader, he was responsible for the "Altnaveigh Massacre" of six Protestants, allegedly in retaliation for the rape of a pregnant woman. Another viewpoint was that his team specialised in killing off duty soldiers. In July 1922, he was captured and jailed in Dundalk prison. 10 days later, he was broken out and soon returned to seize the prison, the neighbouring military barracks, and the town. His next incarnation came as a politician after his election to the Irish Parliament in 1923. He held many positions of power and was responsible for Ireland's strict neutrality during World War II – angering both the US President and British Prime Minister at once. An engineer at heart, Aiken spent his spare time as an amateur inventor – designing a turf-burning fire, spring-heeled shoe and even a beehive. Aiken is a hugely divisive figure in the history of 20th-century Irish politics. He was also the first signatory to the Nuclear Proliferation Treaty in Moscow in 1968.

A widely respected, despised, feared, and stubborn politician, Aiken became the Republic of Ireland's Minister of External Affairs in 1957. He immediately spoke out in favour of nuclear disarmament at the UN's session that year, and it became his life's work. Aiken was almost permanently resident in the UN for over 20 years and spent 11 of them writing draft motions, overcoming rejections, and detailing resolutions involving years of negotiations to deliver the binding NPT resolution in 1968. The LAWS process has been ongoing since 2013, and its difficulties are why I believe it is likely to take at least until 2025, co-incidentally the same timescale as that of the NPT. Cynically, it is altogether probable that LAWS may not be outlawed until all major countries have their own AI weapons so that they can stop proliferation once they and their allies have access to them. Getting a LAWS NPT enacted into international law will likely require dogged determination from the most iron-willed , even controversial diplomats of our generation. Frank Aiken championed the NPT, and Princess Diana was the global figurehead and voice for banning landmines in the 1990s. Who is leading the fight against Lethal Autonomous Weapons today?

A successful treaty would stop the flow of potentially dangerous AI technologies into the wrong hands, ensuring their peaceful use and not in any way that could lead to an AI war. Inspired by the Articles of the NPT, I would recommend the inclusion of various requirements:

1   Parties should negotiate in good faith on effective measures relating to the end of an AI arms race and complete AI LAWS disarmament as soon as possible
2   Each country party to the agreement should agree to forbid the direct or indirect flow of AI LAWS technology or control of such technology to any actor who may intend to misuse it in warfare.
3   Parties should agree not to directly or indirectly receive these technologies or attempt to control them. They should also agree not to design, manufacture or acquire them.
4   Parties should agree to adhere to safeguards designed to redirect AI technology away from ethical applications and toward potentially harmful applications.
5   Parties should ensure that, under international observation and procedures, any potential benefits of ethical applications of AI LAWS technologies are made available to all countries at cost level only
6   Parties must adhere to an independent inspection process to audit any autonomous AI systems, including those that could have dual-use for military systems
7   Five years after the treaty enters into force, parties should meet at a conference to review its progress. They will repeat this every 5 years. The meeting will be the parties opportunity to propose any changes necessary, to be decided by a majority.
8   Twenty-five years after the treaty enters into force, parties should meet at a conference to decide whether it shall continue in force indefinitely or extended for an additional fixed period, to be determined by a majority.

MEDIUM TO LONG-TERM MILESTONES (2025–2030)

1 Educate the World to Understand and to Work Alongside AI
2 Reskilling the Existing Workforce
3 Manage Economic Consequences of Artificial Intelligence

EDUCATE THE WORLD TO UNDERSTAND AND TO WORK ALONGSIDE AI

Education is the most important thing we do. Educating children is how we shape our societies and cultures. School and university curricula are, by definition, what we believe are the most important things that we can teach our children. Learning is also a lifelong pursuit, and learning at home or work is essential as we spend 40–50 years after formal education learning in the workplace. There are five primary users of education or ongoing learning: Children, Workforce, Educators/Teachers, Business leaders and Governments. What each user group has in common is that they do not understand the scale of the impact AI will have on their lives.

Business leaders and experts help governments by providing insights into the future of industry. All G7 governments have created AI breakthrough funds, and their commitment to education focuses on workforce development and University education. Examples include government-funded PhDs in the UK, business-funded AI 'chairs' in US universities and funding workforce training in the UK, Germany, Russia and China. Business leaders worldwide are lobbying governments for support, funding and contracts relating to AI. Business Leaders and government appear to anticipate the coming change, but they are not sharing that knowledge clearly enough for the rest of us to understand.

Governments around the globe are driving change now in tertiary education. Universities are increasing numbers of Data Science and AI courses at Degree and PhD level. There is also growth in short-course and 1-year Masters courses in relevant AI topics. However, one critical omission is the education of school children. If you are 5–10 years old, by the time you enter the workforce in 2030–2035, AI will have removed some roles from the jobs market and, more crucially, **reduced** the number of positions available in many more. For example, we will not need as many middle managers as data will make it easier to manage large teams. **We need schools to communicate with parents, to enable them to help their children think about new careers**. The days of parents pushing their children towards 'doctor, accountant, architect, lawyer' will already be in sharp decline by 2035. It's time we told the world that the future is different. It is the government's responsibility to broaden the debate about AI into schools and homes so that we can prepare the future workforce as early as possible.

RESKILLING THE EXISTING WORKFORCE

Another group of users is the existing workforce. Reskilling the current workforce is vital, and governments play the most significant part in supporting local economies through change. This is probably the most important group, as workers are the tax payers, parents and community leaders – the glue of our communities and engine room of our countries.

One recent historical example of a dramatic shift-change in the jobs market is the UK coal mining industry. The UK was the first country in the world to industrialise – the coal mine literally powered the Industrial Revolution, driving growth and invention that fuelled other sectors, such as shipbuilding, steelmaking and construction. From 1760, the coal mining industry prospered for 200 years, however, increases in manufacturing costs and new alternative energy sources in the 1960s and 1970s meant structural change was coming. These changes and associated government policy saw the UK coal mining industry decimated in the 1980s. Between 1980 and 1987, the coal mining industry lost 152,000 jobs: 68% of the UK coal industry workforce. The Mining Strikes in the 1980s saw entire communities battle against the government for what they believed was their future. Governments promised support and regeneration as the coal mines were closed. Significant support for new industries, inward investment, and targeted the local financial support was given to areas impacted by the closure of the mines. This funding continued for decades. However, reading 'The State of the Coalfields 2019' by Sheffield Hallam University makes for some pretty grim reading. 30 years after the coal mining industry was largely closed, compared to the UK as a whole, former coal mining communities have fewer jobs, lower quality employment and are less healthy, leading to shorter life expectancies. If considered together as a cluster of 5.7 million people, the former mining areas of West Yorkshire, Nottinghamshire, Durham/Northumberland, South Wales, and Ayrshire would probably be the most deprived region in the UK.

If AI has a similarly catastrophic effect on the jobs market, we need to be ready for that transformation. Starting by identifying the most at-risk roles and mapping skills (and people) to complementary roles will help direct our investments in reskilling and inward investment. This planning is a simple first step that also helps aligns educational efforts at school and university. The next step is to commit to reskilling people just in advance of when the new skills are needed. This level of strategic workforce planning is a discipline used by all big companies and done incredibly well by large retail companies and the military. We should use their expertise to help us plan for the AI shift-change, as for example, it hasn't worked for the former coal mining towns.

MANAGE ECONOMIC CONSEQUENCES OF ARTIFICIAL INTELLIGENCE

Historically, a handful of companies always tend to come to dominate an industry. In previous generations, each country, region or state had its own local winners, e.g., local telecoms, energy suppliers and super-markets. Over the last 30 years, the financial benefits of company scale have seen increasing market consolidation. Regional suppliers such as BP, Deutsche Telecom, EDF Energy or Walmart have scaled and acquired to become international companies. In the Internet Age, the ability to win and serve customers globally concentrates the world market-place in fewer hands than ever. The US stock market has not been so dominated by one market sector since the late 1960s, with c.25% of the stock market weighting in just five companies: Facebook, Apple, Microsoft, Amazon and Google. These companies are also placing big bets on AI and, if successful, it is logical that they will continue their growth and profitability. The resulting market dominance and the potential emergence of Mega-Tech creates bigger potential challenges for society.

Trying to determine the impact of AI on the future economy is what economists call 'long range forecasting.' Disclaimer – for every economist, there is an equal and opposite economist! As I said earlier, experts tend to agree that as AI becomes a mature technology, it will displace physical jobs with virtual labour at a gallop. On the credit side, AI will boost overall productivity, so tax receipts from Corpora-tion Tax will increase. The new jobs created by AI will, on average, be more skilled than those lost, so be more highly paid.

However, there will be a consequent reduction in overall tax rev-enues globally. This 'tax gap' is already in evidence, albeit on a much smaller scale. Like all global digital-first companies, the six Big Tech companies all follow current accounting rules, which result in low Corporation Tax bills in countries based outside their US home base. It is estimated that these six companies collectively save around $10 billion annually, outside the US, on their global tax affairs. $10 billion is a great amount of money but not a significant sum when considering that the UK alone collected $850 billion in government tax receipts for 2019. Introducing specific regulation for Big Tech to increase Corporation Tax take is worth less than a 1% increase in income tax rates of **one** G20 country. This is not a financial game-changer, and under current pre-AI economic models, it is not a significant problem.

Problems will start when we see the job losses from structural economic change brought about by AI. In OECD countries, Corporate Tax is, on average, only 3.5% of total tax revenue (rising to 9%–10% in the UK or Germany). Even using the higher 10% figure, revenue from Corporate Tax is dwarfed by the 24% of income from Employment Taxes and Sales Tax. So, the real challenge for governments will be the domino effect of losing both Corporate Taxes AND the reduction in employment and sales taxes due to mass unemployment. Suppose we forecast that AI could reduce up to 30% of tax earning jobs by 2035. In that case, we can confidently predict that government income will nosedive at the same time unemployment and welfare benefits spend sky rockets in the other direction.

The job losses and tax reduction do not seem to stack up against the predictions of AI increasing GDP. There are two insights here. First, overall global GDP is likely to increase but the wealth gap between rich (employed, AI-skilled, working in Technology) and poor (unemployed/with no AI skills/working in repeatable/process-driven jobs) will widen. Growth in GDP will be more significant in countries where Mega-Tech is based, deepening global inequity. Second, GDP increases do not necessarily lead to increases in government tax collection in all countries.

As an aside, there is one feature of the current tax system that is driving robotisation. Capital investment, e.g., investing in robots, hardware and equipment, is tax-deductible. However, in many countries, investing in training for people is either limited or not tax-deductible. So, companies are incentivised to increasingly automate processes and receive taxable benefits to improve the quality of their machinery but not their people!

It is a skilled financial, political and intellectual feat to predict an industrial revolution's future with any real confidence or success. Perhaps AI's next job. But, we can reckon that by early-2020s, governments will have already started to change the way they tax Technology firms. Assuming that the US and China continue to dominate AI investment and monetise the product innovation that results, today's Big Tech companies (alongside some newer Chinese joiners) will become Mega-Techs. Mega-Tech companies will become increasingly influential both financially and politically. In the 2030s, Mega-Tech could become more prosperous than some nations and have no legal requirement to help the very countries (except their home country) from where they generate their income.

FUNDING THE JOBS GAP

A Digital Services Tax (DST), led by OECD, is the global response to the new economics of internet business. The main stumbling block to agreement is that the US has not wanted to participate, believing that US companies are being discriminated against. US companies dominate the tech sector and will be significantly impacted by the reduction in global profits this would bring. Frustrated with the deadlock, numerous European countries, including the UK, France and Austria, have decided to introduce their own DST. The most common model introduced is to tax profits of digital companies who have a high global turnover; say 2% of companies with turnovers over $500 million. These country models are similar to the proposed global DST, which protects small companies, while recouping some tax.

New tax ideas need to be prototyped and tested ahead of the structural economic change brought about by AI. The concept of DSTs will be needed, especially as more companies digitise and it becomes harder to separate 'mass from scale' – the ability of companies to grow globally without the need for large workforces in local countries. Minimum Corporation Tax is another option. By creating a global minimum level of Corporation Tax in each country, all countries can participate in the future wealth of AI. The 2021 agreement for a 15% corporation tax is a possible turning point in the debate. It becomes harder to move profits between jurisdictions if the base level is the same. As with any new tax legislation, it will take a few years to understand how it will work in practice. One other far-sighted tax planning idea is the Windfall Pledge. Designed by the Future of Humanity Institute, it envisages a future scenario where Mega-Tech companies use AI to dominate the world economy. These companies pledge to give a percentage of pre-tax profits if they earn more than 1% of the world's profit. Currently, no company meets the threshold, and, for example, Apple has around 0.06% of the world's profit. We would need to see a company 16× more profitable than Apple before this kicked in. So, we are a long way from this happening and there are issues with a top-down approach. What if companies don't sign? It is unlikely that companies will sign this pledge unless their competitors do. And if they do, how is the money apportioned; on a global basis? Liberal companies may object to funding countries with repressive political approaches. If forced to comply, companies could either restructure to become smaller or just spend more money to reduce their profitability. Even at a superficial level, this approach has many pitfalls. However, we need to consider this type of visionary thinking to ensure that we do not become a world of AI haves and AI have-nots.

How a government funds itself and our public spending is a critical macro-economic question that we need to address. But people want to know if AI replaces their job – how will they live? The most commonly held approach to funding the AI jobs gap is to introduce Universal Income (UI). Universal Income is where everyone of working age is paid a fixed salary with no obligations to do anything in return. It is different from current social welfare payments based on conditions, e.g. claiming unemployment benefit, needing housing support or child support. Sometimes wrongly labelled as Communist, Universal Income is different; the state pays the salary, but companies and individuals generate taxable revenue for the government – property and business are not centralised. After an initial surge of interest in the 1960s and 1970s, then a pause for a generation, Universal Income is having a renaissance. Amazingly, Universal Income draws support from both left-wing Marxists and right-wing Capitalists for different reasons. Activists like Andy Stern, who authored *Raising the Floor* believe that Universal Income could bring people in poverty up to a decent standard of living. In contrast, Milton Friedman, one of the most famous free-market capitalist economists, also advocated UBI as part of a negative income tax.

Universal Income is not a new idea, and there are even some tenuous examples from Renaissance Europe. However, UBI was truly recognised as an established concept in the 20th century. In 1962, economist Milton Friedman wrote about negative income tax. Robert Theobald's book, *Free Men and Free Markets* followed a year later. Theobald was an intriguing character. Born in India in 1929 to a British business person, he was public schooled in England (which he hated), then joined the army. After demobbing, he studied Engineering at Cambridge, which he soon realised wasn't for him and was advised to take Economics because 'he liked people.' After graduation, he moved to Paris to work with his wife at the Sorbonne, where he stayed for 3 years.

In 1957, they moved to the US, and he began to study at Harvard. Like a modern start-up entrepreneur, he soon got an idea for a book, persuaded someone to pay him $2,000 and left university life. One book led to another, and the marketing for his co-authored 1964 report 'The Triple Revolution' was so successful that it was printed on the front of the New York Times! He followed this in 1966 with 'Guaranteed Income.' The concept caught on, and in 1967 Martin Luther King became an advocate, mentioning it in one of his speeches. A man schooled in the sunset of the British Empire became a 60s pop economist and (almost) inspired the US government to promote guaranteed income legislation in 1969 before it was stopped in the Senate, never to be revived.

Since then, Universal or Basic Income has been trialled in over 20 countries and across all continents. The goal of programmes to date has been to help people out of poverty or learn what works to improve their social welfare systems. Evaluating the many Universal Income tests is tough – each experiment is run differently, with varying levels of income, duration and test groups. For example, in Alaska, an annual payment (between $400 and $2,000) is given to everyone; in Kenya, it is distributed to selected impoverished villages, and in Manitoba, Canada, $1,300 was given to selected households. Because we can't compare the data, there is no definitive answer that can either wholly prove or disprove its success. A lack of a common research methodology is a biggest problem, meaning that we don't have large sample sizes in a consistent format. In fact, many of the examples cited are not really Universal Income at all but more like one-off bonuses. Despite this, we can still get insight into user behaviours or preferences from small sample sizes and there is a raft of positive reporting from UBI schemes. These have included reductions in crime, increases in entrepreneurialism and improved physical and mental health.

The most statistically robust experiment is Finland's Basic Income programme of 2017–2018, which ran nationwide, was mandatory, paid regularly and had a control group. Managed by Kela, the social welfare department, the Finnish experiment paid a basic monthly income to 2,000 randomly selected unemployed people. The test group did not need to do anything to receive their payment, whilst the control group had to look for work and engage with their local welfare office. After 2 years, the participants were surveyed, with some interviewed. The results shared by Kela showed that economic outcomes did not significantly change. There was an additional 6 days a year (7%) increase in employment but it wasn't statistically significant enough to be explained by the data. Many critics of Universal Income believe that it will cause laziness – but this data tells otherwise. The funds were given to a group of people, the unemployed, where accepted stereotypes believe are disengaged or lazy – and the results showed there was, at worst, no reduction in productivity and at best an increase.

There was also a promising positive impact on mental well-being. For those on Universal Income, their happiness levels went up, and those with feelings of depression saw them reduced by 23%. Although this did not lead to any noticeable differences in physical health; however, it may be that 2 years of basic income can't reverse pre-existing health conditions. The test subjects also reported higher levels of trust in people and government than the control group. This finding is interesting as the only real difference between the test and control groups was that the test group had no strings attached to receiving their funds. Just trusting people might not motivate them to find a paid job, but it definitely makes them happier.

Universal income is highly fashionable and is the go-to answer for solving the AI jobs problem. It is a highly contentious subject and, depending on what level you set the income, a costly option. If we think back to AI-led jobs reduction, once most jobs are removed from the market, then the support for a Universal Income would become louder than ever. Other options include continuing existing social welfare systems or Universal Basic Services (UBS). UBS is where basic services, such as transport, communication, education, health, are provided free of charge to the individual. The UBS concept is relatively new and needs a lot of further work; it is a far more complex tool. For example, you would have to decide which services should be included, and then to what level. As a top-down answer which plans resource centrally, it is prone to wastage where people don't use the services provided or change their behavioural patterns. 1970s Communist Russia was not known for its innovation and economic growth.

As well as being an economist, prolific writer and speaker, Robert Theobald was a believer in people and he was not afraid to agitate for change when he felt the political classes wouldn't listen. He was also prescient about technology and communications. The conversations about universal income in the 2020s are almost identical to his works published 60 years earlier. In one of his interviews in the 1960s, Theobald said that he didn't want to talk about guaranteed income. Until the world was ready for it he believed that there was no point. It may be that his works are coming back to fashion and it's time to talk about Universal Basic Income.

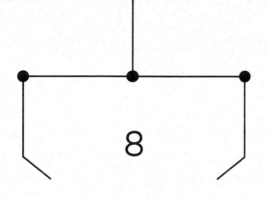

8

A NEW HOPE FOR ARTIFICIAL INTELLIGENCE

...say not, 'How do we find jobs for everybody?' but 'How do we find purpose and meaning and rights to resources for everybody.'
Robert Theobald, 1996.

In the previous chapters, I have used the 'Future back methodology' and described how to align on the current state of AI evolution, look at the options for the future, and create a roadmap. But now, I want to discuss some cause for optimism, because if we effectively manage the challenges of AI, there are great benefits for humanity. A lack of motivation is something we can all understand. There are days when we just can't force ourselves to tidy the garage, when we sidestep that run we promised to do three days ago or find an excuse to avoid that relative that we just don't really like. Many people make a daily living by motivating the unwilling – be it personal trainers, life coaches or your diet coach who tries to stop your cheat day from becoming a week. Far fewer people specialise in purpose. And most of those are philosophers, social scientists or self-appointed 'influencers.' That's because our purpose is more profound, more intrinsic and harder to find and pin down than motivation. Why do we get up in the morning? Why do we go to work every day for a job we don't enjoy? Why do we want to raise a family? Asking these big questions about purpose is the story of life.

DOI: 10.1201/9781003267003-8

From Confucius in the 5th century BCE to Kant in the 18th century, philosophers have debated the purpose of life, and we continue to ask questions today. Religion has driven much of the intellectual thinking on purpose; from sun-gods to roman deities to monotheistic gods. Since the reformation, as Christianity split asunder and opened itself up to fresh ideas, new schools of philosophy blossomed. Eastern philosophies of Confucius or Buddha are now more readily available through global communication. Contemporary philosophers have access to ancient Eastern and Western ideas, resulting in many different theories of what life means. If asked, most of us don't follow a rigid philosophy but we know what motivates us or gives us purpose daily. Purpose is different for everyone. Some people need meaningful work, and others focus on their family or friends. Many people express their purpose through religion or spiritual beliefs. As leisure time increases, sports and hobbies give an increasing number of people their purpose. Some find elements of meaning in all these aspects of life, and purpose can also change as we age and discover new experiences in our lives.

Having a sense of purpose is not only for individuals. We also generate meaning as part of a larger collective. Collective purpose can be as simple as taking part in a local club or group, supporting a basketball or cricket team. Organised religion and successful companies both create a common purpose that binds their members together. Shared prayer has been the foundation of established religion for thousands of years, usually accompanied by a book of religious teaching. A successful business invariably has a clear purpose or vision, to which its strategy is aligned. Companies also create written values, and most have their own distinct culture from which they recruit, manage and reward people.

For individuals, work is probably the single most crucial factor for how people get purpose on a day-to-day basis. In 2019, according to the OECD, the average person spent 1,726 hours at work every year. The only thing we do in our lives more than work is sleep.

As we spend so much time at work, we often build shadow 'work families.' We make friends with colleagues and customers, and many romantic relationships start with an introduction at work or through friends from work. Work is vital for many people to derive their sense of purpose. But when your life's purpose comes from work, when that work goes away, it can be devastating. Research shows that unemployed people have much worse mental health than those in work. Unemployment leads to higher levels of substance abuse, crime, and lower life expectancy. Families with a multi-generational history of unemployment have even worse issues in these areas.

If the ability to work is lost, individuals struggle to compensate for it in other areas of their lives. Financial insecurity relating to job loss can lead to a domino effect of problems with family, friends or health. Losing a job, and being unable to get another one quickly, is a recognised gateway to other problems. Financial insecurity creates anxiety and leads to mental health issues and negative changes in behaviour. Increased incidence of domestic abuse, substance addiction and crime are related to financial difficulties and emerging mental health problems. Of course, mental health issues are not exclusively work-based or as a result of unemployment, however, finding yourself without a job is one of the biggest levers for facilitating mental health problems.

Structural economic change is a challenge of an entirely different magnitude. What happens not only when your job goes away but at the same time when all the jobs go away? What if you just can't change jobs, because there aren't any? The rapid decline of the UK coal industry, with 152,000 jobs lost in 7 years in 1980s has seen entire towns across the UK fighting for survival ever since. Suppose, we map former coalfields against results for UK Annual Wellbeing survey results. In that case, we find that a generation after the mines closed, the "Happiness" Index in these communities is significantly lower than the national average. It has been argued that the problems in former coal-mining towns are magnified due to the loss of community and shared experience fostered by working and living together in a physically demanding and dangerous mining environment. This is undoubtedly true. However, I believe that the greater issue is the loss of shared community purpose.

Massive job losses are not a new phenomenon. Depopulation and unemployment go hand in hand. After Rome's population peaked at 1 million people in the 1st century AD, it declined to 30,000 people. It took over 1,500 years to recover its size. Siena is the birthplace of banking, home to the beautiful "liquorice" cathedral and the world-famous Palio horse race. But after being hit by the Black death in 1348, it took 600 years to recover its population. National governments have more ability and interest to redirect investment within their countries, so 21st-century cities can now bounce back a lot more quickly. As the US and Western Europe industrialised before other countries, there are many examples of recent structural economic changes. In the US, Detroit and the 'rust belt' of the Mid-West have sustained lingering economic and societal problems since their car and steel industries declined in the 1980s. The Ruhr used to be synonymous with the German power, steel and chemical industries – North Rhine-Westphalia (NRW) was once Germany's wealthiest state economy. NRW was the economic powerhouse that the rest of Germany looked on with envy. In the 2020s, this region is now home to eight out of ten of Germany's poorest cities.

Massive-scale job losses in relatively short periods create communities shorn of their collective confidence that is hard to rebuild. As local institutions like Britain's coal-mining brass bands or factory football clubs in Germany disappear, the soft bonds of the local community erode. When young people start to leave to find jobs, the 'talent drain' leads to a vicious cycle of fewer talented working-age people leading to a continuous exodus. The old towns and cities become 'feeders' for newly successful urban centres. So, purpose is not just an individual problem. People need shared experiences to connect and remain confident for the future. In today's world, work is the most significant lever we can pull to change people's purpose.

FILLING THE PURPOSE GAP

So, as we have identified, work is at the top of the purpose pyramid in our current world. If Artificial Intelligence (AI) reduces or removes the purpose gained from work, how do we replace it? If we don't need to work, how do we give ourselves purpose? How do we spend the 1,700 hours per year of free time? Outside work, people's purpose focuses on family, friends, spirituality. Hobbies and sport are also great drivers of personal motivation. The Coronavirus pandemic has given us an insight into what this future could look like. Within a year, we moved from a dynamic, always-on, global economy to one with restricted travel and billions of people in local lockdowns. What did we do with our newfound time? One aspect of many people working from home whilst simultaneously online schooling their children resulted in the most time that parents have spent with their children. Although stressful for many, getting more time with their family has been a revelation for many parents – and children. If we think about the opportunity to spend more time with families, we could change our society. Parents spending more time with their children should improve relationships, boost confidence and ultimately, create more opportunities – meaning that their talents would flourish.

As well as supporting our children, we could also find time to care for our parents and other dependents. Particularly in Western societies, we have passed the cost and burden of caring for the old and vulnerable from family to government. As we live longer and the costs of caring soar, our current approach is financially unsustainable. Morally, many other societies may already believe that this approach is bankrupt. Once we remove work from our day, we will have time to care for our aging parents. Excepting situations with severe illness or mental health, is it appropriate to ask other people to care for your own family if you have the time to care for them? It is difficult to argue against home care if you are paid not to work. The potential impact of this change goes well beyond the financial. Better relationships, happiness and health are closely linked to living in a happy environment. Could home-caring en masse recreate multi-generational living again in Western society? Could AI solve the burgeoning social care crisis?

Helping others could easily be extended outside the immediate family unit. If we are freed from paid work, helping neighbours, or local charities becomes possible and desirable. Retirees and part-time workers often find purpose working in their local communities, such as local councils, sports clubs or charity shops. If we are, in effect, able to retire earlier, then we can support our friends and neighbours earlier. This would bring people together at a younger age and increase engagement in the local area. Changing how we live, changes how we live. Commuter towns would have to be re-imagined as people would look closer to home for their purpose. Large infrastructure projects would need to shift focus to address a more locally based lifestyle.

The other side of the coin is that Coronavirus has created record mental health problems. This has mainly been attributed to the stress of working from home, living alone or trying to work on a kitchen table whilst managing squabbling or bored children and dodgy wifi. Poor mental health is not the preserve of the unemployed, as this is a tsunami of the working. Work has changed and to many has become less fulfilling. It has also given people time to think – am I happy? Turnover is up, and company engagement levels are down. Personally, I believe this is a clear indicator of what happens when people lose purpose and communities collectively lose confidence. This is why it is vital that any Universal Income has **some** conditions attached to it. Providing some direction is essential and although, in the short term, people may be happy to have some time to do what they want, over a period of many years, people need purpose.

A GOLDEN AGE FOR HUMANITY

The Singularity could be our next golden age. Periods of great wealth often lead to artistic and creative growth. The Renaissance in 15th and 16th century Europe was initially driven by growth in European trade and then accelerated by wealth generated from the new world. Wealthy benefactors promoted great artists such as Michelangelo and Botticelli. The riches that followed the Industrial revolution gave Georgian and Victorian inventors space and opportunity to create new products, explore science and think up entirely new industries. The billionaires of the 21st century fund great philanthropic works, build spaceships and are increasingly signing up to give away their fortunes. If we are free from the concerns of funding our day-to-day lives, how would we choose to express ourselves? Not many (perhaps any!) of us could paint the Sistine chapel, but we could let loose our talents in art, social media, music, poetry or song. If we think about Malcolm Gladwells' concept of needing 10,000 hours of practice to create expertise, we could welcome a new renAIaissance. Imagine what millions of individuals could create with 1,700 hours of free time per year.

The pursuit of excellence can inspire individuals to greatness, but what excites me is the sense of purpose that comes when we think bigger. I see this whenever I work on transformation projects. When people come together, they invariably create something unique above and beyond their individual contribution. I guess it's the difference between watching a sports match on your TV or being at the event. It's the same event, but one experience is far richer than the other. Companies are well used to creating that group sense of mission to engage their employees, and they always start with the vision. There are some challenges to humanity that look impossible to solve. With time and space given to us by AI, we could ask better questions of ourselves and look to conquer these challenges.

Let's think about developing a new mission for humanity. And there is room for more than one. We are explorers and curious creatures. Space and other planets are obvious choices for new missions, but our oceans, landscapes and our own biology still have many secrets to unlock. We live in a world riven with poverty and hunger, even in the world's wealthiest countries. Some scientists consider climate change to be a potential extinction-level event for humanity. If we could deploy an extra 100,000 people to researching any of these problems or building new technology, would it help? Of course. And by attracting people with a real passion for the mission, we can solve problems and make people happier whilst doing it. This could be the golden age for humanity, where we take the benefits of AI and use it to design a better world. As AI develops, we need to be ready to exploit this opportunity. Although the Singularity will be decades away, and talk of missions seem far-fetched and irrelevant, by using the future-back approach, we design for a future that we want.

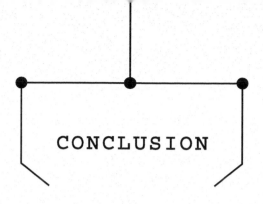

CONCLUSION

'The Moon in the full of night over the high mountain,
The new sage with a lone brain sees it:
By his disciples invited to be immortal,
Eyes to the south. Hands in bosoms, bodies in the fire.'

Nostradamus, The Book of Prophecies, 1555
(Quatrain often cited as the prediction of artificial intelligence)

Artificial Intelligence (AI) is our greatest challenge. As AI evolves into something more significant and profound by the day, it is also perhaps becoming our greatest hope. I am no Nostradamus or time travelling AI from the future (although looking at how loosely the above Nostradamus quatrain predicts the coming of AI, maybe he was no Nostradamus either), but I see AI as a force for good and believe that the world can share in its benefits. Artificial Intelligence is truly godlike, the more I read and listen and watch, the more I realise that I don't truly understand the scale of AI and never will. It's too vast. There is no latter-day Victorian polymath who can comprehend the intellectual vastness of AI disciplines. If there is, that polymath will be an AI.

I am convinced that we will continue to merge with technology – as AI becomes programmed into our everyday lives, it recodes humanity, perhaps one day biohacking into our very soul. The next generation will live through a transformation in how we work, live and think. Of course, we will need to build safeguards to protect ourselves with regulation, policing and taxation. This is normal with any new technology. But more importantly, we will get the real opportunity to decide who we want to be. Do we want to perpetuate the world as it is or design it as it should be? The debate is starting to happen in Big Tech, on university campuses and in governments, but now is time to let the people in and democratise AI. The citizens of the world are the users, and we all need to plan for living with AI.

INDEX

Note: *Italic* page numbers refer to figures.